The Virtues: A Very Short Introduction

VERY SHORT INTRODUCTIONS are for anyone wanting a stimulating and accessible way into a new subject. They are written by experts, and have been translated into more than 45 different languages.

The series began in 1995, and now covers a wide variety of topics in every discipline. The VSI library currently contains over 650 volumes—a Very Short Introduction to everything from Psychology and Philosophy of Science to American History and Relativity—and continues to grow in every subject area.

Very Short Introductions available now:

Available soon:

AMPHIBIANS T. S. Kemp
MODERN BRAZIL Anthony W. Pereira
ARBITRATION Thomas Schultz and
    Thomas D. Grant

BIOCHEMISTRY
    Mark Lorch
PHILOSOPHY OF PHYSICS
    David Wallace

For more information visit our website

www.oup.com/vsi/

Craig A. Boyd and Kevin Timpe

THE VIRTUES

A Very Short Introduction

OXFORD
UNIVERSITY PRESS

OXFORD
UNIVERSITY PRESS

Great Clarendon Street, Oxford, OX2 6DP,
United Kingdom

Oxford University Press is a department of the University of Oxford.
It furthers the University's objective of excellence in research, scholarship,
and education by publishing worldwide. Oxford is a registered trade mark of
Oxford University Press in the UK and in certain other countries

© Craig A. Boyd and Kevin Timpe 2021

The moral rights of the authors have been asserted

First edition published in 2021

Published in the United States of America by Oxford University Press
198 Madison Avenue, New York, NY 10016, United States of America

British Library Cataloguing in Publication Data
Data available

Library of Congress Control Number: 2020945704

ISBN 978-0-19-884537-9

Printed and bound by CPI Group (UK) Ltd, Croydon, CR0 4YY

To Rebecca DeYoung and Aaron Cobb,
whose work and lives exemplify the importance and
admirability of the virtues

Contents

Acknowledgements

The genesis for this VSI came from our earlier edited work, *Virtues and their Vices* (Oxford University Press, 2014) and owes a great deal to the authors who contributed to that volume. We would also like to thank Jason Eberl, Aaron Cobb, and Joanna Boyd-Wilhite for their comments and suggestions on earlier drafts, and to Christian Miller for his insightful input on the manuscript as a whole. Jenny Nugee and Andrea Keegan at OUP also provided invaluable help and guidance for the project.

List of illustrations

Chapter 1
Whose virtues, which vices?

Habits, skills, rules, and virtues

The primary aim of this book is to give an overview of virtue
understood as an excellent way of being. Having the virtues shapes
the patterns of our behaviour. But as these opening pages
illustrate, although virtue influences behaviour it cannot be
reduced to mere behaviour. Virtue involves having certain skills.
But it also requires knowing what the point of those skills is, and
thus knowing when the excellence of a certain skill might require
us to break a rule. In the coming pages, we aim to point out
exemplars that model certain excellences. Those exemplars give us
guidelines on how we should act. But we also show that becoming
virtuous involves knowing what the point of that guideline is, and
knowing when slavishly following the rule isn't the best option.

Consider the case of the would-be chef who begins by following
recipes. The recipe provides rules for how to mix ingredients, how
to treat eggs, grains, vegetables, and spices. It provides rules for
baking, frying, and grilling. It serves as a prescription or guide for
what the beginner should do. But we can also understand the
recipe as a description of what the excellent chef does.

The young athlete who aspires to play in the World Cup practises
every afternoon taking shots, passing the ball, dribbling with both

feet, trapping the ball, juggling, agility, etc. She works under the guidance of her coach who gives her rules for her drills. 'Strike the ball this way, not that way. Keep your head up. Know where to pass the ball. Do not use your toe. Lean over the ball. Move to open space.' These instructions (and rules) are designed to help the novice player learn the skills necessary to play the game well.

To become good at some activity, we need to develop skills specific to that activity. A skill is an acquired ability to perform a specific kind of action in the service of some particular purpose. Baking is a skill a chef employs in the service of eating and in the further service of maintaining one's health or the enjoyment of eating good food with others. Passing is a skill that an athlete employs in the service of scoring a goal for the further purpose of winning a game. Skills are developed by repetition and by following the rules that govern their acquisition. But true excellence is when the skills are internalized and people don't have to mindlessly follow rules or even explicitly consult them.

Experts are people who have internalized the principles of good cooking or good football through years of experience so that they now 'naturally' do these things without explicitly consulting the recipes or the rules. The excellent athlete, like the expert chef, knows what to do, when to do it, and how to do it. They are the people who know that when the rules apply and when they do not cannot be determined by yet another rule. The expert is the person for whom the principles have become a 'second nature'. They have so internalized what the rules aim at, that following them or knowing when in fact to break them, comes to them naturally.

In a similar way to a recipe or instructions from a coach, a moral rule is a description—or an approximation—of what a morally excellent person does that simultaneously functions as a prescription for the novice. The limitations on recipes and rules are that they simply provide guidelines from the perspective of the individual who has not internalized them. Rules may tell us what *to do*; but they don't tell us *how to be* (Figure 1).

One important moral habit is honesty. Parents might have rules that their children 'always tell the truth'. Very young children often come to follow the rules as required by the parents. A child might not know why the truth-telling rule applies but she might follow it as it is possible her life might depend on it. The rule can function to help the young child, and as she grows she comes to see why the rule applies. But as the child grows, her parents want her to not only understand the value of telling the truth, but also to internalize honesty as a valuable character trait.

Like excellent chefs or excellent footballers, morally virtuous people do not slavishly follow rules. Moral virtues go much deeper than providing rules for behaviour and descriptions. Morally good people internalize principles of good behaviour (like truth-telling)

1. **Hercules represents how each person must make the difficult decision between the easier life of vice and the more disciplined life of virtue.**

so that their actions provide a model, or exemplar, for what people should do. That is, honesty can be viewed as a virtue, and not simply as a rule; and we can look to honest people as exemplars for our own behaviour. But what is it about honesty that makes it a virtue? To know how to answer that question, we first have to know the answer to a previous question: what does it mean to *be* a virtue?

The consensus across cultures and traditions seems to be that a virtue is an excellent and stable quality of the soul that enables a person to act well regarding some kind of activity. That is, virtues are 'good habits'. For a quality to be a virtue it needs to persist over time. A one-off action is not a virtue since it is an isolated instance. As Aristotle observes, 'One swallow does not make a spring.' But a virtue cannot be just any quality but an excellent quality. But what do we mean by the phrase 'excellent quality'? In one sense, it means that the quality helps a person acquire some excellent end, like truth-telling or right thinking. But it can also mean that it makes its possessor excellent. In this second sense, a virtue promotes the growth and maturity of its possessor and it will enable its possessor to practise the activity with relative ease and pleasure. Thus, any serious study of the virtues will attend not only to what the virtues are but how we acquire them.

Although many people rightly understand 'virtue' in terms of moral qualities, the scope of the term is wider than that. There are also intellectual and productive virtues. A chef possesses a kind of productive habit but a scientist possesses an intellectual habit. When we possess these habits in an excellent manner, we call them 'virtues'. These cooking and experimental qualities are not, however, moral. The more typical way we understand a virtue is with regard to 'moral' virtue—in the sense that it makes its possessor morally good and it aims at morally good ends or activities.

Just as there are characteristics that are marks of intellectual or moral excellence, there are also characteristics that are marks of moral failure, such as dispositions to dishonesty, injustice, arrogance, and greed. These dispositions to behave badly are the vices. We can see that the criteria for what constitutes a vice correspond in important ways to those of virtue.

A vice, then, is a stable but harmful quality of the soul that prevents a person from acting or living well. Like the virtues, the vices are qualities that endure over time. We expect liars to lie habitually and with relative ease. The habit becomes so engrained that they often do so as a 'second nature'. But lying, like other vices, tends to frustrate real goods we long to possess like community, friendship, and trust. For a quality to be a vice it typically frustrates the ends for which an agent aims or it actively harms the agent. But to understand how vices (and virtues) operate they need to be seen contextually.

Like the broad range of cuisine people might encounter in their travels, the virtues are socially and culturally situated with expert practitioners of their own. Some of the characteristics of virtuous people will vary with place, locale, and historical time frame. But that doesn't mean there aren't such things as human excellences any more than the differences between gelati and pie mean there's no such thing as an excellent dessert. Modesty, for example, might function differently for a Japanese school child (where silence and deference to one's elders take precedence) than it does for an English real estate agent (where a certain amount of confidence and extraversion are critical to their success). But this raises an important problem in our consideration of the virtues: are these qualities so diverse that they really share nothing in common? That is, doesn't relativism pose a problem for any account of the virtues?

Although there are individual, social, biological, psychological, and religious differences among people and their practices, it does not follow that there are no common cross-cultural elements. Theologians and philosophers like Thomas Aquinas and C. S. Lewis insisted on a shared human nature and basic moral principles (e.g. honouring one's parents, practising justice, cultivating wisdom) that were essentially the same throughout the world. More recently, positive psychologists in their empirical research have identified 'the High Six' virtues (courage, justice, humanity, temperance, transcendence, and wisdom) that exist in all cultures throughout the world and over time. Even though the virtues might differ in their expression from one culture to another, they 'have a coherent resemblance to one another'. The reason for this is that values like honesty and compassion are the elements without which no society can function. It may be, as the positive psychologists argue, that we are 'grounded in biology through an evolutionary process that selected for these aspects of excellence as means of solving the important tasks necessary for the survival of the species'. The upshot of this points to a human nature that both the Japanese school child and the English real estate agent share, but one that will also manifest itself differently given unique social and cultural locations. So despite the variation, the virtues can be understood as creating and describing an ideal account of what it means to be a morally good person in diverse cultures, religions, and philosophical traditions.

An important quality differentiates athletic and artistic qualities from moral virtues. Lionel Messi or Julia Child may (or may not) be morally good human beings. A person can be a great athlete or a great chef (i.e. they may possess excellent skills essential to the practice of their profession) while also being a morally depraved human being. Conversely, a virtuous person might have no artistic or athletic abilities or skills. What we see, then, is that there may be an analogous way of acquiring skills, character traits, abilities, and virtues, but the nature of these qualities differs radically. A moral virtue, in the words of philosopher Robert Adams, is an 'excellence in being for the good'. And this good is not merely the athletic or culinary good, but the moral good.

Orienting oneself towards the good requires that we stop any harmful habits and begin the cultivation of a new set of excellent habits. Ignatius Loyola (1491–1556) was a mid-career soldier in Northern Spain who had a life-altering experience. He was an excellent soldier and he had seen himself as a stylish, handsome man. And by his own admission, he was a person who was excessively concerned with making a good impression in the courts of the local Spanish nobility. But in a battle at Pamplona in 1521, a cannonball crashed through the castle wall he was defending and broke his leg. The doctors set the leg incorrectly. It had to be reset more than once, and at one point some of the bone had to be sawn off. While he was convalescing at home, he wanted to read some books about knights and their heroic deeds. But none could be found; so he settled for books on the life of Christ and the saints. The more he read the more he was intrigued and thought to himself, 'I could become a saint. And I should become one if I can.' So, he began a long process of character transformation from a narcissistic soldier to the altruistic saint who founded homes for prostitutes, schools for the poor, and missions for the sick. By the end of his life, he had cultivated habits of compassion, self-discipline, humility, and perseverance.

The discipline necessary to becoming a good soldier was analogous to those disciplines necessary to becoming a good person. A helpful way to think of Ignatius' virtues, and indeed the virtues in general, is to consider them as a 'second nature'. Just as we all possess a given nature by our genes, we can also acquire a second nature in terms of our personal qualities, dispositions, and behaviours. No one is born with an ability to speak Italian or play the cello, or to practise self-discipline, or to act justly. But given the relative psychological and physical malleability of human nature, most people can acquire them.

A person acquires these abilities over time, with practice, and under the supervision of someone who already knows the language or the instrument. In time, a person can converse in Rome or play a Mozart quartet with relative ease. So, too, the person who practises self-control over her desires for, say, coffee follows a similar pattern. Suppose the person thinks it's best to not drink more than an entire pot in the morning. At first, it's hard for them to resist. They love the taste of coffee, and they're used to it. But the more they cut back on their intake, the easier it becomes to resist the desire to overly caffeinate. Furthermore, having others to help encourage them and hold them accountable will increase their chance of success. If they practise self-control long enough, they may find not only that their behaviour has changed, but that it is now 'natural' for them to do this in their revised morning routine.

These acquired patterns of behaviour lead us to expect people to behave in predictable ways. But more importantly for virtue, the internalization of the pattern changes persons themselves. A virtuous person enjoys doing virtuous things and experiences a kind of moral disgust in the thought or performance of a vicious act. As the chef finds the poorly made dish disgusting, so the virtuous person finds the immoral act repulsive.

Like virtuous people, vicious people also behave in predictable ways. However, the vicious person pursues the goods of food, drink, sex, status, excellence, and property in inappropriate ways. A vice is a habitual disposition to act in ways contrary to what the good person would think, do, and feel. For example, wrath runs contrary to the patient, thoughtful, compassionate concern of the virtuous person by a habitual surrender to violent and uncontrolled outbursts of anger. Moreover, the vicious person enjoys what she does. Instead of experiencing sorrow or disgust at engaging in bad behaviour, the truly vicious person enjoys it. The wrathful person feels justified and satisfied in the expression of their anger. But just as there are different lists of the virtues, so too there are different lists of the vices. Since the vices are opposed to virtues, we should expect this; what one thinks is vicious depends on what one thinks is virtuous. A fairly standard list of the vices emerged in the early era of Christianity and still resonates with many philosophers, psychologists, and theologians.

Among the lists of vices seven are understood as 'capital' (from the Latin *'caput'* for 'head'). This list includes pride, envy, avarice, wrath, sloth, lust, and gluttony. These vices are all ways in which people pursue the various goods appropriate to human beings in ways that are harmful to themselves and others. Each is an improper orientation toward a good that a virtue aims at. They are dispositions to behave in predictable ways with the accompanying affective responses. The proud person enjoys looking down on others; the wrathful person takes pleasure in recklessly venting her anger; and the slothful person enjoys avoiding the demands his relationships require of him.

Many of the virtues, therefore, can be understood not only as those dispositions that help us to resist the lure of the vices but also as ways of developing healthy attitudes towards our desires. A virtue, then, is not merely an acquired ability to act in *any* predictable way, but one that helps us pursue the good in the right way and with the appropriate affective dispositions. The fully virtuous person takes proper delight in the exercise of the virtues (Figure 2). For those of us who do not find virtuous activity delightful, this reflects the fact that we are not complete in virtue.

Consider what it means to be a gracious person. At the end of the year, your workplace gives awards to various employees. The gracious person (as distinguished from the polite person) not only offers congratulations to those who get the awards, but she also does it in a predictable way with kind words. Yet, there is also another hidden quality, this affective disposition of gladness for the other person which the polite-but-not-gracious-person does not have. Buddhists call the affective disposition to delight in the other person's good fortune *muditā*. The truly gracious person—the person who has *muditā*—not only does the right things but also feels the right emotions in the practice of virtue.

2. Medieval art often depicted the nature of the virtuous life in terms of trees with roots, trunk, and branches that were all part of an organic unity.

A short history of thinking about the virtues

Although we can trace the origins of the virtues back in the West to Plato, Aristotle, and the Stoics, we can also find them in the various religious traditions of Judaism, Christianity, Islam, and Buddhism—among others. A common theme is that they all appealed to the idea that people should develop stable dispositions that assist them in pursuit of a good life.

The virtues receive the greatest attention from philosophers in the thought of Aristotle and Thomas Aquinas. The *locus classicus* for the virtues is in Aristotle's (384–322 BCE) *Nicomachean Ethics*, which is a compilation of student notes from his lectures. It lacks the polished quality of a finished treatise but nevertheless provides reference points for how we still think about the virtues. Of particular importance are his definition of virtue and the role of virtue in human flourishing. Aristotle defined virtues as certain kinds of human excellences that help us 'to live, think, and do well'. There are, then, three broad categories of virtues that he lays out for his readers: moral virtues (which help us live well), intellectual virtues (which help us think well), and practical virtues (which help us make things well).

The artisan who cooks well has the practical virtue of art, where art refers to anything a person can produce well, ranging from cooking and painting to architecture and poetry. Art is an excellence a person possesses that enables him to take various raw materials and transform them into something new. The excellent abilities of the artist imbue the artefact with an excellence the novice does not have. A Picasso or a Julia Child possessed the virtue of art in ways that others do not. Art, therefore, is a kind of 'knowing how to make things'.

Since we also are creatures who not only need to make things well, we also need to think well. That is, we need virtues of the mind, or 'intellectual virtues'. These virtues of the mind facilitate everything from daily decisions about whether a politician's statements are truthful or not to the practices of scientists in their laboratories about how to test a specific compound. But these excellences are not strictly moral qualities. There are those who are great thinkers but who also possess bad character. In order to flourish we need to not only be able to make things well, and to think well, we need to be able to act well—and it is this acting well which is the domain of the moral virtues and leads to human flourishing.

The moral virtues, on Aristotle's account, played the central role in a life of flourishing. The Greek word Aristotle uses for 'flourishing' is *eudaimonia*. But it has often unfortunately been translated into English as 'happiness', which is a notoriously slippery word whose meaning can range from an emotional state of contentment to something much more robust. Rather, flourishing indicates an overall and fairly constant sense of well-being.

The moral virtues enable us to control and shape our appetites so that we are not merely subject to the whims of unrestrained desires. Reflection shows us that unbridled desire does not lead to a flourishing life. The greedy person does not flourish; her life isn't going well as a whole because she is incapable of controlling her insatiable desire for ever increasing amounts of wealth. Aristotle would say she cannot flourish precisely because she lacks virtue. A good person not only needs to be able to think well about her actions, she also needs to be able to control her appetites and act with courage based on what she knows. Courage, as one of the moral virtues, helps to show how the moral virtues require a kind of consistent overcoming of various desires that might lead us to choose the easy course of action rather than the more difficult route that leads to a life well-lived.

Aristotle's teacher, Plato (429–347 BCE), also addressed the virtues, most notably in his work *Republic*, where he sees justice, wisdom, courage, and self-control applying to both the human soul and the state itself. For Plato, we could divide the soul into mind, a 'spirited element', and the appetites. Wisdom was the virtue of the mind, courage of the 'spirited element', and self-control of the appetites. For Plato, justice had a kind of priority and applied to the overall harmony of one's soul: that is, when wisdom (with the assistance of courage) ruled the appetites.

Like Plato, Cicero (106–43 BCE), the great Roman statesman, saw the virtues as central to the life of civic responsibility. Without the virtues, neither the person nor the state could flourish. For him, all morally right action springs from four particular virtues (prudence, justice, courage, and self-control), which have come to be called the 'cardinal' virtues. In Latin, *cardo* means 'hinge' or 'that on which a thing turns'. And so the cardinal virtues are often seen as the main virtues that both individuals and states need to flourish. Other virtues can be seen as further specifications of these four. As Cicero describes the cardinal virtues, prudence is 'the full perception and intelligent development of the true'. Justice preserves society itself by 'rendering to everyone what is their due'. Courage is the 'strength of a noble and invincible spirit'. And temperance is the 'orderliness and moderation of everything that is said and done'.

Augustine (354–430) inherited Plato's understanding of the virtues as mediated through Cicero. In his early work Augustine praised the four cardinal virtues and then later wrote on the theological virtues of faith, hope, and charity, which could only be acquired by divine grace. In his most mature work, *The City of God*, he sees the cardinal virtues as fundamentally flawed unless they are corrected and reoriented to God by the theological virtues. He says, 'For although some suppose that virtues which have a reference only to themselves, and are desired only on their own account, are yet true and genuine virtues, the fact is that even then they are inflated with pride, and are therefore to be reckoned vices rather than virtues.' Pagan virtues, even those that facilitate peaceful coexistence and social harmony, don't have their orientation in God and thus, in his view, are not genuine virtues.

Thomas Aquinas (1224–73) inherited the philosophical tradition of Aristotle through Islamic thinkers like Ibn Rochd (1126–98), Jewish thinkers like Maimonides (1138–1204), and other Christian thinkers like Albert the Great (1200–80). But looming behind all these was the figure of Augustine and his interpretation of the Christian faith. Standing in the Christian world of Augustine and the philosophical world of Aristotle, Aquinas attempted to incorporate the Aristotelian account of the virtues into a wider theistic understanding of the moral life. He characterizes the virtues not only as good for living a well-ordered life here and now with regard to thoughtful and peaceful coexistence with others, but also in terms of an explicit appeal to God. He says, 'Virtue is a good quality of the soul, by which we live rightly, of which no one can make bad use, which God works in us, without us.' Like Aristotle, he sees virtue as a good quality of the soul that makes both the person and her action good. But he also sees it as having its ultimate origin in God. The Good Samaritan practises compassion not only because he may have empathy for the wounded traveller, but more importantly because compassion for the stranger is a direct reflection of his love for God and all those made in the image of God. Yet more importantly, Aquinas also thinks that the Good Samaritan is only able to love the other because God enables him to do so. That is, the Christian virtue of charity enables a person to love even his own enemies as Christ commanded his followers to do in the Gospels.

This virtue of charity stands out in Aquinas's thought as a particularly striking example of his use of Aristotle in the service of his Christian account of the virtues. In the *Nicomachean Ethics*, Aristotle devotes great energy to a discussion of friendship as central to a life of flourishing. Aquinas then integrates Aristotle's idea of friendship into his own understanding of charity as a 'friendship with God'. Even though this would be impossible for Aristotle to consider—since friendship can only be between equals—Aquinas contends that we love the friend (i.e. God) for the friend's *own sake*. Yet, we also love those whom the friend loves. Suppose we have a dear friend who has children. We have never met the children, yet we love the children because we love our friend. Aquinas suggests that we can even love our enemies because of our love for God—who loves *all* people. Charity, therefore, is a kind of universal friendship for all people based upon a love for God.

But one shouldn't think, from these examples, that the virtues are only important for figures in ancient Greece and Rome or the Christian West. In ways similar to Judaism and Christianity, the cultivation of a morally good life plays a central role at the core of Islam. The understanding of ethics differs in different strands of Islam. But for all of them, the virtues are important. The Arabic word for Islam, إسلام, means 'voluntary submission or surrender to Allah (God)'. And although this might initially seem to be primarily about behaviour rather than one's inner character, a closer examination shows that in Islam the outer and inner cannot be separated so easily. The term 'Muslim' comes from the same root as 'Islam' and means 'those who submit' to Allah. But this purification is not just a purification of behaviour. It is a complete purification of action, thought, desires, and dispositions. One cannot become the kind of person that Allah calls one to be without becoming virtuous. Islamic reflection on the virtues also makes a central claim found elsewhere, and that is that vicious people harm themselves. The Qur'ān repeatedly claims that sinners *anfusahum yaẓlimūn*, that is, that they 'wrong themselves' or even 'ruin themselves'. But just as importantly, Allah is often described in terms of the virtues. Allah is among other descriptions merciful, compassionate, just, and honest.

A focus on the virtues can also be found in the philosophical and religious traditions of the East. Like Plato, Aristotle, Augustine, Ignatius, and Muhammad, Confucius (551–479 BCE) was concerned with virtue. He understood *dao* to be the right way or path that a good human life should take and on which society should be structured. 'What is the *dao* [way] to be a good person?'

Confucius asks. His answer lies in cultivating *de*, which means a 'good moral character'. And a good moral character, as we have seen, is how virtue has historically been understood. Virtue, or *de*, is thus required if we are to achieve *dao*. More specifically, Confucius thought *dao* requires us to develop *ren*, which is translated as 'benevolence', 'goodness', 'virtue', and even 'complete virtue'. Prior to Confucius, *ren* primarily referred to a quality possessed by aristocrats. But, for Confucius, it became a moral excellence that anyone who applied themselves could achieve.

Confucius' advice on developing *ren* parallels Aristotle's thought in a number of ways: a focus on moral education or cultivation through practice, the importance of social customs, the training of emotions, and even something that looks similar to Aristotle's doctrine of the mean and the importance of exemplars. However, the different contexts in which Confucius and Aristotle lived also result in a number of important differences. (One important difference is that the primary source of Confucius' thought on virtue, the *Analytics*, was written not by Confucius himself but rather is a collection of sayings attributed to Confucius by his disciples. The *Analytics*, in this way, also lacks the systematic nature of Aristotle's *Nicomachean Ethics*.)

We see then that for many centuries across a wide range of cultures, philosophers and theologians focused their attention on virtues, their descriptions, and their acquisition. But in the West with the advent of the Protestant Reformation and the rise of modern philosophy, virtue came to play a less central role in ethical thought. Protestant religious figures like Martin Luther (1483–1546) and John Calvin (1509–64) emphasized faith and obedience to the commands of God (similar to what we saw above in Islam), but apart from these two virtues—and occasional appeals to love—very little was said about other virtues in terms of their role in the daily life of the average person. Theological disputations over grace and faith took centre stage and discussions concerning the nature and acquisition of the virtues seemed to sound too much like a 'works-based righteousness'—something the Protestant Reformers found heretical.

For the philosophers of the modern era, the virtues were relegated to a secondary status and replaced with rules, commands, consequences, and rights. David Hume, Immanuel Kant, and John Stuart Mill, for example, all addressed the virtues, but they never saw these qualities of the soul as anything more than helpful auxiliaries to their own already developed moral theories which were based upon moral sentiment, universal duty, or net utility respectively.

In the work of David Hume (1711–76) we see an approach to ethics that emphasized moral sentiments and enlightened self-interest. Hume rejected the traditional list of virtues and instead offered one where the virtues were those qualities we cultivated to make our own lives—and the lives of those we live with—more pleasant. For Hume, virtues were simply qualities that led to a more pleasurable life while vice frustrated that goal. They were, at best, instrumental goods.

More sympathetic to the traditional virtues than Hume, Immanuel Kant (1724–1804) saw duty—as determined by reason alone—as the locus of ethically right action. In determining how we should act, we need to think in terms of rules of action that apply to all people universally and necessarily. Yet, if we performed our duty because the act brought us pleasure or because it accomplished some purpose other than duty for its own sake, it could not qualify as a morally praiseworthy action. Virtues, then, had to serve the purpose of duty, even if we all have a duty to develop virtue.

Although John Stuart Mill (1806–73) devoted much of chapter four of *Utilitarianism* to virtue, he saw it as subordinated to net utility and his general happiness principle. People do not naturally desire virtue but if they can be induced to see it as pleasurable (and vice as painful) they can begin to understand that a virtuous life can contribute to the overall happiness of society. Yet Mill says very little about the specific virtues, how we should acquire them, or whether we should desire some virtues more than others. Hume, Kant, and Mill can be understood as engaging the virtues but not to the extent that they contribute much to the wider conversation.

How the virtues work

We intend this book as a work about the virtues themselves, not about constructing various theoretical frameworks for the virtues (i.e. 'virtue theory'). However, there a number of ways to approach virtue ethics. And among these competing theories, the ones that have carried the most influence are those developed by Aristotle and Aquinas. An Aristotelian–Thomistic account of the virtues is one that emphasizes that the virtues function both in terms of being important elements that lead to a good life (what philosophers call 'instrumental goods') and also as qualities that we desire for their own sake (what philosophers call 'goods in themselves'). That is, the virtues function as a way of achieving happiness, or *eudaimonia*. Philosopher Philippa Foot contends that an Aristotelian–Thomistic account of the virtues is still the best starting point for conversations about which lists, what kinds of virtues, what kinds of vices, the role of the virtues, and how people come to acquire the virtues. But two other views of the virtues also should be included and engaged as they offer complementary (and sometimes competing) ways to consider the virtues. The first approach, offered by philosophers like Linda Zagzebski, is called 'exemplarist' since moral exemplars play the central role. The exemplarist approach places a priority on how the virtuous person would act. Although *eudaimonia* is an outcome, the virtuous person as model is key to the exemplarist account of the virtues.

When confronted with a difficult moral problem, people have asked questions like, 'What would Confucius do? What would

Muhammad do? What would Gandhi do? Or what would Jesus do?' This approach emphasizes the good person not only as the standard by which we should think about morality but also sees the person as an exemplar to be imitated. Just as we become better chefs and athletes by imitating Julia Child and Lionel Messi, we become better people—morally speaking—by imitating truly virtuous people.

The exemplarist approach appeals to Aristotle's idea that in order to become virtuous we should imitate the exemplar not only with regard to the actions themselves but the manner in which the exemplar acts. We should not start with a theory about morality and the virtues but with imitating the good person. That is, a person might not initially understand how it is that virtue contributes to flourishing or how it is constitutive of the good life. Although we begin with simple imitation we should come to the point where we internalize the right affections with regard to our actions; and we do this by performing an action *as the good person would perform it.* Mother Teresa's observation that 'Not all of us can do great things. But we can do small things with great love' captures the exemplarist idea that both action and the manner of action are important. The truly compassionate person not only relieves the suffering of others but does so in a way that she empathizes with the other person.

The overwhelming success of 'self-help' books points to the fact that people are not only dissatisfied with their lives, they also see some of their own desires and drives as morally problematic. People buy books to control their food cravings, to become more efficient, to overcome alcohol and drug addiction, and to be mindful. They don't buy books to become morally worse. We realize that we are often more tempted by harmful habits than by healthy habits. In fact, it is absurd to think of being 'tempted' by good habits unless one already possesses them or somehow catches a glimpse of their allure in the midst of a life of frustrated vice. The magnetic pull of the harmful seems to be greater than the lure of the good. The vices often seem to be more prevalent than the virtues.

The second approach goes back to Plato, and is defended in recent work by philosophers Iris Murdoch and Robert Adams. The Platonist sees the virtues as ways of moving out of the confinement of our own selfishness and morally bad behaviours. 'The Good' provides us with a vision that calls us to a better life. Again, this may be a happier life but only because we have developed virtues that help us renounce our former ways of immorality.

This Platonic approach to the virtues begins with the basic intuition that the self and its destructive desires must somehow be overcome. Plato's 'Allegory of the Cave' shows that all people are imprisoned in their own ignorance and their ignorance of The Good causes both evil and suffering. Knowledge of The Good frees us from the shackles of ignorance and the suffering caused by ignorance and our undisciplined pursuit of desires. In Plato's cave people are chained and see only shadows on the wall, but they assume the shadows are reality. But the philosopher—the one who is a lover of wisdom and of the good—breaks free from the chains, stands up, turns around, and sees that the shadows are caused by images being placed in front of a large fire. He then moves beyond the images and the fire to the entrance of the cave. He moves outside into the sunlight—but his eyes must adjust to the bright sunlight. He sees the true things themselves—not the images—and he understands that they are all illuminated by the Sun—Goodness Itself. But this process is painful. To develop a good character, to understand and be transformed by one's union with The Good, means to move past the inertia of our moral selves and to pursue the good relentlessly. And most people do not possess these qualities.

Like Plato, Iris Murdoch sees the self and its desires as obstacles to the development of virtue. Yet, she sees humility as a key virtue since it resists the wanton arrogance and self-promotion that we are naturally inclined to pursue. She says, 'Humility is a rare virtue and an unfashionable one and one which is often hard to discern. Only rarely does one meet somebody in whom it positively shines, in whom one apprehends with amazement the absence of the anxious avaricious tentacles of the self.' The self—and its vices—must be overcome by the practice of virtue. And humility is the key.

In this context then, we can distinguish between the acquisition of the virtues as central to living a good life, providing exemplars for how we should live, and as a call to being better people than we currently are—or even calling us to renounce our evil patterns of behaviour. But these features are not necessarily in conflict with one another. As the chef and footballer analogies illustrate, all three of these aspects can be seen as connected. The difference among these three approaches is thus often one of emphasis rather than specific content.

In the following chapters, we aim to illustrate how specific virtues contribute to the good life directly, apart from a justification via rule-following. These virtues include what we would call moral, intellectual, and theological virtues—as well as those virtues that can help correct the more serious vices. The virtues are important since they (1) facilitate the attainment of happiness, and (2) reveal themselves in morally mature persons who can—with the proper training—be imitated. Like the good chef and the good athlete, the good person—the virtuous person—embodies values in ways that transcend merely following the rules. But throughout our focus is on specific virtues understood to be at the very foundation of ethics and the good life.

Chapter 2
The moral virtues: feeling good about being good

The moral virtues

Suppose you find a magic ring—one that makes you invisible. Do you use it for your own advantage, do you refuse to use it seeing it instead as a temptation to evil? Or do you use it for some other purpose? Both J. R. R. Tolkien, author of *The Lord of the Rings*, and Plato consider this problem. Both claimed that the great majority of us would eventually use such a ring for our own selfish purposes. Very few of us would resist for very long; the temptation would lead us to compromise our character. What could we do, like Sam Gamgee, to resist the call of such power?

In order to think clearly about this particular issue as well as other moral problems we need to understand how 'good moral thinking' works. Practical wisdom is the solution because it also helps us attend responsibly to issues of justice, courage, and self-control. These four virtues—often known as the 'four cardinal virtues'—play a central role in most lists of the virtues since Plato and Aristotle first offered their own accounts (Figure 3). These virtues are 'cardinal' in the sense that the other virtues 'hinge' on them. Medieval theologian and philosopher Thomas Aquinas described the cardinal virtues as the 'chief' virtues since they 'especially claim for themselves what commonly belongs to all virtues'. As Aquinas understands the cardinal virtues, they contain the

3. This book cover of Orby Shipley's sermons represents, in pictorial form, the interlocking nature of the cardinal virtues.

common qualities of all the moral virtues since each of the cardinal virtues perfects one of the various capacities of the soul. The other virtues are subordinate to one of the cardinal virtues; for instance, patience is subordinate to the cardinal virtue of courage. Since, for Aquinas, patience is the virtue to suffer well evils or hardships inflicted on us, it is closely connected with courage, which deals with enduring the danger or risk of death.

In a scene from the movie *Gladiator*, a dying Marcus Aurelius (played by Richard Harris) tells his son Commodus (played by Joaquin Phoenix) that he will not rule Rome after Marcus' death.

'Rome is to be a republic again'. The elderly Aurelius declares that Commodus is not fit to rule because he does not possess the four cardinal virtues. Commodus, however, claims that he has other virtues: ambition, resourcefulness, devotion. What Commodus does not realize is that ambition itself is not a virtue, since one can have ambition for bad aims. In fact, Commodus' ambition 'goes too far' and he suffocates his father to assume rule of Rome. Resourcefulness too can be used for bad ends. Commodus practises resourcefulness as he murders his father for the sake of his own ambitious and wicked purposes. The same is true of devotion; it is a moral liability rather than a benefit if what one is devoted to is not morally good, such as Commodus' illicit devotion to his sister Lucilla. Commodus' ambition, resourcefulness, and devotion could have been virtuous, but only if they were to align with the cardinal virtues since these virtues guide us to morally good ends.

As we consider the four cardinal virtues, there are a range of human emotions, desires, and motivations—like ambition, resourcefulness, and devotion—that will be virtuous only if they're aligned with these virtues. The cardinal virtues are often seen as perfecting different parts of human nature so that all the virtues can be seen as falling under or largely shaped by one of the cardinal virtues.

Aristotle describes prudence, or 'practical wisdom', as 'right reasoning about what is to be done'. For him, it is the most important of the cardinal virtues since it has all human activity under its purview. No one can be virtuous without deliberating well, judging well, and choosing well concerning any course of action. Justice is the second most important virtue and involves 'giving to others what they deserve'. But of course, rendering to others what they deserve depends on prudence in knowing who the person is, what my relationship to that person is, what they are owed, and how I ought to give what is owed. The final two moral virtues are fortitude and temperance. Fortitude, or courage, concerns our 'fight or flight' emotions. It helps us to do the 'difficult thing' that we struggle to face. And temperance, or self-control, helps us to moderate our desires for food, drink, and sex. Discussing these four virtues in greater detail will also help establish a more general framework to understand the moral virtues more broadly.

Prudence

Prudence is chief among the cardinal virtues given that all human activity falls under its guidance. Prudence is unique among the cardinal virtues in that it is the only one of the four that functions as an intellectual virtue. This description, however, might suggest that there is a stronger disconnect between the intellectual and moral virtues than there really is. Plato thought that all the virtues were unified in that a person who has one of the cardinal virtues has them all. And since he also thought that knowing the good always leads to doing the good, in a sense all virtue is unified in wisdom as a kind of intellectual excellence. He thus didn't draw a sharp divide between intellectual and moral virtues as others in the tradition have done.

As an intellectual virtue, prudence helps us think clearly and rightly. But it's a specific kind of intellectual virtue aimed at acquiring morally good qualities. Prudence, as Aristotle puts it, helps us 'deliberate finely about things that are good and beneficial ... not about some restricted area ... but about what sorts of things promote living well in general'. An important part of prudence is having correct perception about the situation—'seeing things as they are and what's demanded of us', we could say. Prudence helps us see what the other virtues require of us. It helps us track the morally relevant features of the circumstances, and determine how our actions ought to be sensitive to the salient elements of the situation. Suppose, for instance, that Allison wants to be a responsible consumer. Although she loves her morning double-shot Americano, she also wants the coffee farmers who grow her beans to be remunerated well and to minimize environmental damages that her (and others') drinking habits contribute to. This inclines her to buy only fair-trade certified coffee. But then she comes across a newspaper article arguing that fair-trade certification contributes to uneven economic advantage for farmers and doesn't actually result in the environmental benefit that she initially thought. What should she do? Figuring out this kind of thing is one of prudence's roles, because it is 'right reason' about the various factors that enter into our deliberation. Prudence not only guides us in terms of *what* we should do, but also shapes *how* we should be motivated by what we should do.

According to Aristotle, merely reasoning in accord with right reason isn't enough for prudence. One must reason in this way *because* it accords with right reason for the agent to have prudence. That is, a person needs to be able to know what she should do but she must also feel the right way about the action. Prudence is the ability to think through a proposed course of action in terms of deliberating about the various circumstances and what might happen. It also judges about what she should do and when she should act. Yet, simply being able to think, judge, and act are insufficient. A person needs to be able to do this in a way that is motivated by the right moral considerations and properly enjoy being responsive to them. For this reason, Aristotle says that even though a person needs prudence to think correctly, she cannot truly be virtuous unless her appetites are also well ordered. An integrated person is one who thinks well, feels appropriately, and acts rightly.

Various vices will make it harder for an individual to have prudence. Consider again the case of Commodus. His excessive ambition distorts his view about what he ought to do, enabling him to engage in the self-deception necessary to think that he deserves to rule Rome. Likewise, 'craftiness' is not the same as prudence. Craftiness involves knowledge about what deceptive or counterfeit means will achieve a particular end, even if that end under consideration is a genuine good.

So prudence helps us deliberate well about the various goods. But it also helps us know how to achieve the good ends of the other virtues. As Aristotle puts it, the other virtues set their proper goal, but prudence tells us how to properly achieve those goals. This is why, in Plato's *Republic*, the political rulers must be prudent. They set up the educational system that is to train the citizens in virtue. Prudence requires us to know the proper kind of musical, physical, and emotional education that Plato thinks is required for the well-functioning *polis*. It's not surprising, then, that he devotes two of the ten books to the qualities that good rulers should have. For if, Plato argues, the rulers are not lovers of wisdom, then 'cities will have no rest from evils'.

Aquinas affirms Plato's insight and goes so far as to develop 'political prudence' as the most important species of prudence since the ruler has the care of the entire political community, like a mother or father of a family. The good ruler not only deliberates, judges, and chooses well on behalf of himself, but also on behalf of the entire *polis*. And this lack of prudence is why Commodus, especially, would be unfit to rule Rome.

Temperance

The second of the four cardinal virtues is temperance. If prudence perfects us with respect to the intellectual faculty, temperance is the virtue that perfects us with respect to the bodily appetites or desires—and especially the bodily desires related to food and drink. While the Stoics think that the virtues are sufficient for flourishing, others in the tradition (such as Aristotle) think certain further goods are needed as well. For these thinkers, food and drink are obviously essential goods for human flourishing. We cannot flourish—that is, we are not living well—if we are severely malnourished or dying of thirst. But there are ways to be oriented toward food and drink that contribute to our flourishing, and there are ways to be oriented toward them that detract from our flourishing. Once we see how temperance is understood as excellence with regard to the bodily desires for food and drink, that understanding can also frame how we think about other desires, such as the desire for exercise, the desire for physical rest, the desire for sexual pleasure, and even perhaps the desire for leisure activities such as tennis or wine-tasting.

Aristotle thinks that temperance is best understood as a mean or midpoint between two extremes, and the pattern here holds for other virtues regarding our appetites as well. He describes the moral virtues as 'consisting in a mean, the mean relative to us, which is defined by the reference to right reason...It is a mean between two vices, one of excess and one of deficiency.' The person who desires food or drink too much is not a temperate person. 'Eating indiscriminately or drinking until we are too full is exceeding the quantity that accords with nature...That is why these people are called "gluttons", showing that they glut their bellies past what is right; that is how especially slavish [to their bodily desires] people turn out.' Nor is the temperate person the one who desires food and drink too little. While this orientation does not have a common description that parallels the use of 'glutton' for the person excessively disposed towards the good of food and drink, the person who does not properly value this good also fails to flourish. What Aristotle articulates here is that the mean as 'relative to us' is not that the nature of the virtues is relative in the sense of there being no objective fact about what the mean consists in. Rather, it is the point that the objectively right amount of food, and the right desire for food, will depend on specific facts about the person. The marathon runner will need more food for daily activities than will the otherwise sedentary academic. And so we do not consider the runner gluttonous for eating a quantity of food that would be so for the academic.

Because moderation with respect to desire is at the heart of temperance, it is sometimes understood as a general rather than a specific virtue. Aquinas, for instance, describes temperance and fortitude as general virtues as follows: 'temperance withdraws a person from things which seduce the appetite from obeying reason, while fortitude incites a person to endure or withstand those things on account of forsaking the good of reason'. That is, in the general sense we can think of temperance as the generic virtue that keeps individuals from being seduced away from right reason, and fortitude in its general sense as the generic virtue that enables us to endure difficulties in pursuing what right reason tells us to achieve. Understood in this way, all moderation can be seen as a kind of temperance. The intemperate person is the one who is overly disposed towards pleasures and pursues them at the expense of other, more important, goods, for example, people who spend too much of their income on concert tickets and do not save either for emergencies or retirement. But more specifically, temperance deals with moderation with regard to food and drink. It is this more specific sense of temperance that is considered a cardinal virtue.

If temperance is excellence with regard to the desire for food and drink, the excellence here can be seen as having narrower or broader scopes. If the good that food and drink aim at is just bodily health, then the relevant excellence would be excellence in promoting health. Any desire to eat or drink beyond what is needed for health, on this narrow understanding, would be contrary to the virtue of temperance. However, on a broader understanding, there are other goods that food and drink aim at besides just health. For instance, a fine single malt scotch shared with a colleague after the completion of a project or a glass of Malbec enjoyed with a friend at the end of a long and demanding week. Neither is, strictly speaking, needed for health. But there are social goods that such drinks can promote. It is in the service of these goods that Aquinas says that the proper use of intoxicants can be 'most profitable' and drinking in moderation can be good for 'the joy of the soul'.

A similar point can also be seen if we return to the broader, more general understanding of temperance. Virtuous sexual activity will depend on what we take the good, or goods, of sexual activity to be. If the good of sex is limited to the good of procreation, then this narrow understanding will put constraints on which sexual desires align with right reason; that is, on this view consensual sex with no intention to procreate would not qualify as virtuous. If, however, there are other additional goods that proper sexual desire aims at, such as intimacy, then a wider range of sexual desires will be consistent with general temperance.

Note here, too, that temperance does not only address our bodily actions. That is, temperance is not primarily about what we do or do not eat, what we do or do not drink. Rather, temperance is about our inner disposition toward food and drink. Bradley Cooper's character, Jackson ('Jack') Maine, in the 2018 remake of *A Star is Born*, is an alcoholic. But he's an alcoholic even when he is not drinking. Jack doesn't become temperate simply because there's no liquor around since he drank it all the night before. This is also why we shouldn't confuse eating disorders with a deficiency of the desire for food and health. Eating disorders are primarily about control and only secondarily about the pleasures that come from food. Temperance isn't primarily about restricting or restraining our food consumption, as in the case of anorexia; it's rather about a positive appreciation for the good. The temperate person does not have to resist the temptation to over- or under-eat precisely because they do not have that temptation. Their desire is not contrary to right reason because it is shaped by right reason. In fact, we should resist seeing illnesses like anorexia or alcoholism as instances of intemperance, since such conditions are better characterized as involving illness rather than vice.

Every temptation toward gluttony thus affords us an opportunity to develop self-control and become temperate. Since developing temperance involves training our physical desires, it might be hard to see how we can do this since our desires are not under our direct control. Suppose, for instance, that you recognize that exercise is good for you but you do not regularly do it. You do not enjoy it, though you wish you did. After all, finding pleasure in exercise would make it easier to motivate yourself to exercise. You cannot become the kind of person who likes to exercise by a simple act of will. How then do you become the kind of person who likes exercising? The answer is by exercising. Of course, one single swim or jog or game of squash won't do the trick. You will need to exercise repeatedly over an extended period of time. Each time you do, it will become slightly easier to exercise the next time (once your muscles are no longer sore, that is). And if you do it long and regularly enough, you just might discover that you have, over time, become the kind of person who no longer hates exercise. You might even discover that you have come to enjoy exercise. This is the process known as habituation. And it's the same process by which we form the moral virtues. You can train yourself over time to like coffee (or scotch or tofu) as you train your palate and come to appreciate more what you are consuming. But our bodily desires are also shaped by how we think about them, not just the bodily sensations that they involve. In thinking about how meat is produced, for example, we might find the process so horrific that the thought of eating it disgusts us.

Courage

Our desires are not the only human capacity that virtues can perfect. Humans are beings with desires; but we're also emotional beings. And much of what is true about temperance being the virtue that moderates our bodily desires is also true of virtues that moderate our emotions. The third cardinal virtue, courage, is a virtue involving the perfection of the emotions—specifically the emotion of fear. And if we think of the cardinal virtues as each perfecting a particular kind of human capacity, we can understand the range of virtues related to the emotions as subordinate to courage.

The emotion of fear is, in general, intrinsically a good thing, even if not every instance of fear is good. It's part of our natural 'fight or flight' response to perceived threats. A few years ago, one of us was hiking in the Smokey Mountains. After a long hike, I was changing out of my hiking boots in the parking lot when I spotted a black bear at the edge of the parking lot. I walked over a bit closer to get a picture. Another hiker came up to me and asked, 'Aren't you scared to be this close?' No, I answered. She followed up: 'Do you know how fast a bear can run?' This gave me the opportunity to say: 'I don't have to run faster than the bear. I just have to run faster than you.'

Fear quite literally can save our life. Fear is good. Not feeling fear in the face of a real threat to our health, our family, or livelihood is bad for us. We sometimes ought to feel fear, even if that fear doesn't change how we act. But that doesn't mean that fear is always good. We can be afraid of the things that don't pose a real threat to us. We can be afraid of something that ought to cause us fear, but feel too much of it. We can be paralysed by our fear rather than motivated by it. The fear of hardship may keep us from working hard enough to accomplish some of our goals.

Malala Yousafzai (Figure 4) is a young woman born in 1997 in the town of Mingora, Pakistan. During her early years, the Taliban fought to take control of the area and implement their extreme views forbidding women and girls from going to school. Malala saw this injustice and became a vocal opponent of the Taliban by arguing that all people—not just men and boys—have a basic right to education. As her popularity grew, so did the opposition of the Taliban and so they issued a death warrant against this 14-year-old girl. But she persisted in her advocacy. Malala remarked that 'we were scared, but our fear was not as strong as our courage'. Her courage did not eliminate her fear; she was afraid and rightfully so. Rather, her courage enabled her to control her fear, to keep it in its proper place. The next year, as she was riding the bus to school, a masked Taliban gunman boarded the bus, identified Malala, and shot her in the head. She was taken to a nearby hospital and treated. She recovered and continued her advocacy,

4. Malala's courage in the face of death threats helped open up the possibility of education for girls and women in her community.

eventually becoming the youngest person to win the Nobel Peace Prize. Malala is brave because she habitually faced threats against her life with resolve, and her bravery enables her to do courageous acts. Her resistance to religious intolerance and institutionalized sexism is born from a courageous character and not merely an isolated anomaly. Malala's actions are courageous because they spring from a character that is *consistently* courageous. Her courage is a persistent form of human excellence that enables her—and others—to live better lives.

Although numerous philosophers have thought that courage primarily deals with fortitude on the battlefield, it can also be seen in the face of any threat to one's life or well-being broadly construed. Malala's continued work for women's education, in the face of death threats from the Taliban, arguably involved being in a war zone. But her courage also consists in showing that the Taliban's fear was misplaced: 'The extremists are afraid of books and pens, the power of education frightens them. They are afraid of women.' Their fear of education for women shows that they are not properly oriented to the communal good.

Those who, like the Taliban with respect to education, fear too much are cowards. But others who fear too little in the face of a real threat are foolhardy and rash. Both extremes signify vice since they both depart from a 'mean'. But even when we feel the proper amount of fear, it should not overtake us. That is, it should not prevent us from doing what we need to do. Furthermore, to be truly virtuous our courage needs to be in the service of good ends. Aristotle captures many of these elements in his summary of courage:

> Whoever stands firm against the right things and fears the right things, for the right end, in the right way, at the right time, and is correspondingly confident, is the brave person; for the brave person's actions and feelings accord with what something is worth, and follow what [right] reason prescribes.

We also see here that courage promotes confidence, where we do not let fear control us. The virtue of courage is not simply about the emotion but about what we are able to do when we feel that emotion. Here, too, we see how the intellectual virtue of prudence is needed for us to know what and how much we ought to fear and helps us discern the proper response to such fear. Sometimes, we ought to stand our ground. Other times, we should flee.

There are also similarly structured moderating virtues for other emotions, with a vice of excess and a vice of deficiency. Both too much and too little anger are vicious, while the virtue involves feeling just the right amount of anger as called for by this situation. Something similarly is arguably true of sadness as well. Interestingly, Aristotle thinks that the emotion of shame doesn't fit this pattern. Aristotle thinks of shame as a kind of 'fear of disrepute'. We feel shame when we are disgraced by what we have done. But the truly virtuous person, Aristotle thinks, wouldn't need to feel shame since 'we think it wrong for him to do any action that causes a feeling of disgrace'. Shame is, he thinks, at best a 'pseudo-virtue'. However, if we take seriously the claim that the virtues are dispositions to feel emotions at certain times, a person could be disposed to feel shame appropriately even if they never do in fact have the occasion to feel it because they never do anything shameful.

Justice

Of the cardinal virtues, it is the last of them that causes the most disagreement about its nature. Justice creates difficulties not only about its definition but also about the scope of its application. While prudence, courage, and temperance all seem to be focused on individuals with respect to their deliberation and control of various emotions, justice is fundamentally social. And since we are beings who must live in society, justice tends to cover a wide array of issues ranging from taxation and fair wages to restitution for property damages and freedom of expression.

What we see at work here is the assumption that we truly do have obligations to others, and the reason we have these obligations is that others have value independent of me and my interests.

Kantians, utilitarians, natural rights theorists, and virtue ethicists all assume this to be the case, although the reasons why a person has value will vary accordingly. Regardless of the source of this value (in Aristotle, it is because we are social, rational beings who must live in community; but for Aquinas it is because we are beings made in the *imago Dei*), the value of the other is the source of obligation to that other person. And so justice is that virtue by which we treat others according to their value. Further, since we are beings who by our very nature are social, justice stands as one of the most important of the virtues; every interaction with another human being can potentially be understood in terms of justice.

Plato and Aristotle saw justice as descriptive of both individuals and the body politic. More recently, modern and contemporary thinkers like Locke, Marx, and Rawls saw it primarily in reference to society. For Locke, justice consisted in respecting another's natural rights and the government's protection of those individual rights. For Marx, it was taking from each according to his ability and giving to each according to his need. For Rawls, justice was fairness in the process of the organization and arrangement of social and economic goods. But for both Plato and Aristotle, it was rendering to others what is their due, or what is owed to them. And for these two ancient philosophers, justice applies to our relationships to one another as well as to the larger society. In order to understand justice as giving to others what is their due, it can be helpful to think of it in terms of three different forms: legal justice, distributive justice, and commutative justice—moving from more minimalist accounts to the more expansive.

The first form of justice is legal justice. We are obliged to obey the laws of the state (assuming they are just laws) but all this requires of us is an outward act of justice. I pay taxes, I serve on juries, I obey speed limits if I drive, and I keep my dogs from irritating the neighbours. But this does not require an inward disposition of any kind since I may resent paying my taxes or obeying the speed limits with my car. We see here in legal justice a requirement of obedience to the law that aims at the common good of society— nothing more. This is a kind of bare minimum of justice. But if I am to keep the laws of the land, the government also is obligated to me. And this is known as distributive justice.

The social whole, that is, the state, owes me protection of my rights as a citizen which include my rights to my life, my property, and access to any other goods necessary to my well-being. For the state to incarcerate me without due process or to take my land for a government building without compensation or consent is a violation of distributive justice—even if that action happens to be legal and thus satisfies the stricter legal justice. The state— considered as the *res publica*—owes me protection and retribution if necessary. Again, here, since the state is not a person per se, it cannot have dispositions to regard me and mine in ways that reflect true virtue. To consider justice truly, we need to see it in terms of how it actually manifests in real persons.

Commutative justice is what I owe another person considered as a person. That is, the relationship of person to person serves as the model for all the forms of justice in terms of what we owe others as having the same basic value that we possess. For example, my colleague at work is owed honesty, respect, professional deference, and consideration. And she owes me that as well. For her to lie about me violates justice since her action actively takes from me what is owed to me as a person deserving of respect—it could even result in the loss of my job. But I encounter others not only as individual persons, but as fellow members of larger communities that are owed things in virtue of being part of those communities.

In all three forms of justice there is an integral social element of indebtedness to others. Not only must we refrain from harming others, but we are also obligated to assist those in need. That is, we are to respect others. In thinking about this, we could consider the story of the French village of Le Chambon-sur-Lignon during the Second World War. The village became a haven for Jews escaping Nazi persecution. Villagers would hide families in farms, houses, or secret places in the mountains in order to save them from deportation to the extermination camps. What is remarkable about this is that the entire community participated in the scheme to save lives. Not only did they see the persecution of Jewish emigrants as a violation of justice, they saw that their own refusal to save innocent human beings would also be a violation of justice.

But in the practice of justice, the individual must also possess a disposition to practise justice—not because of kinship or friendship, but because in justice we encounter the other person as another person worthy of our moral concern, rendering to her what she is due regardless of special relationships. The villagers in Le Chambon shared neither religious identity nor kinship with the Jews they saved. Yet they treated them as persons deserving of respect and dignity. And they chose to act courageously because it was just—despite the Vichy government's capitulation to Nazi practices and the law as it then stood. As thinkers from Augustine to Martin Luther King, Jr have noted, an unjust law is no law at all.

The cardinal virtues, as the central moral virtues, help us develop those qualities that enable us to think and act well across a broad spectrum of relationships. In helping us to consider ourselves in relationship to other people, justice not only helps us act towards them as we should, but also facilitates us in doing this in the right manner with the right attitude. So, too, courage and temperance help us not only guide our desires and fears but to do so with relative ease. These cardinal virtues can—by extension—shape other subordinate virtues like modesty, honesty, and generosity. But in all the virtues, prudence—as 'right reasoning about what is to be done'—will serve as the touchstone for how a person cultivates the right course of action and the attendant affective attitudes.

Chapter 3
The intellectual virtues: being mindful

Moral and intellectual virtue

Virtues are specific kinds of excellences. Some acquired abilities, like the virtue of art, require an intellectual as well as a practical ability in order to transform various kinds of materials. The virtue of prudence is understood as practical wisdom about what ought to be done morally. It directs us toward the other virtues in two important ways. First, it helps us see how other virtues contribute to an excellent human life. Second, it instructs us how to go about forming and exercising those virtues. Both of these roles can be seen with the analogy to cooking. True excellence with regard to the culinary arts requires right reasoning about what one ought to cook or avoid. Cooking well involves reasoning well about the ends one ought to achieve with one's cooking—such as nutrition or gustatory pleasure. The outcome of this reasoning will also depend on context, as the BBQ pit-master will reason differently from the committed vegan. But cooking excellence also requires knowledge about how best to transform one's raw materials into the selected dish. We fail to be prudent when we do not properly understand the goal of the good life, when we are wrong about what traits contribute to our achieving such a life, or when we are wrong about the means to developing those traits in order to flourish. In this way, there's an intellectual component to developing any of the moral virtues. And since prudence is an intellectual virtue, a cardinal virtue, and necessary for the moral virtues, the boundary between intellectual and moral virtues is somewhat blurred.

Yet other kinds of excellences primarily concern good habits of thinking about the world. They involve certain skills and habits in reasoning and how we approach our beliefs. These intellectual virtues help us think clearly about what truly is the case and help us to discover things we previously did not know, even apart from shaping our actions. (Though they ought to do that too.) Another way of putting this is that the intellectual virtues are habits of the mind that facilitate the pursuit of truth, the avoidance of error, or other epistemic goods. Conversely, intellectual vices are habits of the mind that frustrate these goals. And it is possible that a person with intellectual virtue might not necessarily possess moral virtue.

Galileo seemed to possess a number of important intellectual virtues (Figure 5). He was curious about the movement of the planets, he was creative in terms of thinking about alternative

5. Galileo offers an exemplar of intellectual courage and perseverance in the face of considerable institutional opposition.

models, he demonstrated persistence, he showed intellectual courage, and he had mastered the various forms of scientific demonstration known to 17th-century natural philosophers (which is how the 'scientists' of the day were known). The fruits of his intellectual excellences were many. And yet, he seemed to lack some of the moral virtues. He was arrogant, impatient, and lacked discretion in how to engage others in positive ways. Galileo's arrogance and impatience, for example, prevented him from seeing the scientific value in the works of Kepler and Schreiner, two of the pre-eminent scientists of the day. Had he taken their work seriously, he would have seen how their efforts could have enabled his own theories to move forward. What Galileo shows is that although there cannot be an identification of the intellectual and the moral virtues, there does seem to be some kind of convergence at key points. If the intellectual virtues have as their aim the discovery of truth, the avoidance of error, or ensuring that we've done our epistemic best, then some kind of value must be placed on the virtues of honesty, curiosity, humility, and perseverance—among others. And this value will not just be for scientists (or natural philosophers), but for all persons.

Intellectual virtue among the Greeks

The belief that there are specific intellectual virtues goes back as far as ancient Greece. The Sophists, whose name is connected with the Greek word for wisdom, *sophia*, were itinerant teachers in the 5th century BCE. They would travel from city to city, presumably training their pupils in *areté*, that is, in virtue or excellence, in exchange for money. Many wealthy families employed the Sophists as a means to political influence. Unlike later philosophers, the Sophists didn't see wisdom as concerned with objective truth for its own sake. The goal was practical—how to achieve political influence through rhetorical ability. One Sophist, Protagoras, seems to have rejected the existence of objective moral norms in favour of what is more useful or expedient. Protagoras, like a number of other Sophists, makes appearances in Plato's dialogues. And although the Sophists' practice was not uniformly problematic, Xenophon, a student of Socrates, captures what many thought of them when he described them as 'speaking to deceive for their own gain'. It is here that we get the idea of *sophistry*.

Aristophanes' play *The Clouds* depicts and mocks Socrates as a Sophist. This association was one that Socrates wanted to reject. When brought to trial for corrupting the youth of Athens, Socrates devotes some of his legal defence, his *Apology*, to distancing himself from the Sophists. Socrates himself left no writings; what we know of him is through the writing of others, especially his student Plato. Socrates, as described by Plato, repeatedly stresses the importance of truth over persuasion, advising the jury to 'pay no attention to my manner of speech... but to concentrate your attention on whether what I say is just or not, for the excellence of a judge lies in this, as that of a speaker lies in telling the truth'. And Socrates described his own teaching as focused on making Athens' citizens 'as good and as wise as possible'. In fact, Socrates taught that knowing the good inevitably leads to doing the good: moral virtue and intellectual virtue seem to be not just related but identical. Wisdom, specifically knowledge of 'the Good', just *is* the whole of virtue.

Plato, like his teacher Socrates, thought that human flourishing, happiness, was attained through the pursuit of virtue. In the *Laches*, Plato says that knowledge of good and evil is the whole of virtue, thereby turning all vice into ignorance. While Plato doesn't always identify wisdom and virtue, he still closely links them. The central question of Plato's *Republic* is why a person should be moral. There, Plato's character Socrates is talking with a number of friends about the nature of justice. Thrasymachus claims that justice is 'nothing other than what is advantageous for the strong'. Socrates counters that justice can't be this, since what is advantageous for the strong sometimes harms other people. And if justice is a virtue, then it can't harm the other. The brothers

Glaucon and Adeimantus question Socrates about why we ought to be just if it doesn't always lead to our own benefit. Glaucon thinks that justice is an extrinsic good—it's only good for us by what benefits it brings to us. Socrates argues that justice is both extrinsically and intrinsically good. To show how justice can also be intrinsically good, Socrates sets out to show, via a very winding conversation, that a person is better off when they're just.

Since justice in the individual is the very same thing as justice in a city, and because justice will be easier to see in the city given its larger scale, Socrates tries to construct a hypothetically flourishing city from scratch. And so we see that in the *Republic*, Plato thinks that when each part of the city does its job or role well, including the rulers ruling with wisdom, then the city will be just. Plato also thinks that justice in the city parallels justice in the individual. So, following the pattern we saw in the city, the wise person who, because of that wisdom, develops courage, will also be just. Justice and wisdom are linked even if distinct. And in the *Apology*, Plato claims that *knowing* the good always leads to *doing* the good. But this seems false. I know that the sixth espresso of the morning is bad for me, that the pleasure isn't worth its impact. And yet I drink it anyway.

Aristotle rejected this tight connection between *knowing* the good and *doing* the good. He distinguishes between intellectual virtues and moral virtues—what he calls virtues of thought and virtues of character respectively. These two kinds of virtues are fostered in different ways, the former by instruction and the latter by habituation. With this distinction, Aristotle loosens Socrates' and Plato's connection between wisdom and virtue as a whole. Aristotle offered five specific intellectual virtues in Book VII of his *Nicomachean Ethics*: *sophia*, *technê*, *episteme*, *nous*, and *phronêsis*. Each of these five is a 'good habit of thinking' which enables its possessor to think well about various topics. The last of these is translated into Latin as *prudentia*. As seen in Chapter 2, prudence is one of the cardinal virtues. His treatment of the other four is rather idiosyncratic, especially given the cultural distance between his context and our own.

While influential, we think the renewed focus on the intellectual virtues and their role in the flourishing life in contemporary philosophy provides a more useful approach. We might think, for instance, that laziness and arrogance—as intellectual vices—often prevent researchers from arriving at the truth. In contrast, diligence, honesty, and humility all seem to be requirements—to some extent—of making significant scientific and intellectual progress. For instance, the Navier–Stokes equations, originally developed in 1822, describe the motion of viscous fluid. Think of how your maple syrup may seem to rotate just slightly as you pour it on your porridge on a cold winter morning. There are situations, however, where it's not clear if the Navier–Stokes equations give the right solutions. Mathematicians have thus far been unable to prove that the equations succeed, despite there being a one-million-dollar prize for success. Kazakhstanian mathematician Muchtarbai Ötelbayev initially thought he'd solved them in 2014 after thirty years of work, but later realized that he'd made an error. Intellectual diligence is a good habit of mind that keeps Ötelbayev working on the problem. Other good habits of the mind include the virtues of intellectual courage, open-mindedness, and curiosity. These intellectual virtues are conducive to or constitutive of the good life for individuals and communities.

Return to the discussion of Galileo. While he displayed many intellectual virtues, his life suggests that he lacked a number of moral virtues. Galileo's example demonstrates that he possesses specific intellectual excellences but also that these good habits of thinking did not entail moral excellences (and we are not suggesting here that he was evil—simply that he lacked some of the moral virtues). But we can still ask: are intelligent people *generally* good people? As we saw in the previous section, if we take 'intelligence' to include wisdom, Socrates and Plato thought they were. Plato's student Aristotle thought a person could know what morality required of them and not do it. So, it doesn't look like being intellectually virtuous entails being morally virtuous. But what about the relationship the other way? Is it the case that morally good people make better thinkers, better scholars, or better researchers? If that were the case, we should expect the best thinkers, scholars, and researchers to be morally good people. But that doesn't seem to be the case either. That is, it doesn't look like being an excellent researcher requires all of the moral virtues. But we might think that being a good researcher requires at least some virtue. Wouldn't an excellent scholar, like Ötelbayev (or Galileo), need honesty, patience, and perseverance? It's unlikely someone could work on a problem with his level of commitment without patience and perseverance. And he admitted when he realized the solution he thought he'd found failed. What about the rest of us? What would it look like for us to have those intellectual virtues that facilitate the pursuit of truth?

Intellectual honesty

Truth is important. Few of us would endorse that a general pattern of active deception is compatible with virtue. We value a commitment to the truth. Sometimes, our lives depend on it. ('Does this vaccine actually work?' isn't something we want to always find out by trial and error.) And much of the time, society at large requires a commitment to truth for commerce, communication, and familial relationships.

But like most things, not all truths are good for all people at all times. A general commitment to the truth does not require we always disclose the true things we know or pursue truths that can be known but are inappropriate to be known. If a stranger asks me for my debit card number and pin, I'm under no obligation from a general commitment to the truth to give it to them. I have no obligation to tell all the truths I know about others. As is evident by recent discussions of privacy with respect to our online data trails, this concern for appropriate disclosure of information will only become more pressing. According to Google's own Transparency report, they received over 121,000 requests from government authorities during 2018 to release data from over 261,000 Google user accounts. That's one request every 4 minutes and 20 seconds.

There is thus a range of different relationships we can have to the truth. We can love it. We can love it but be too lazy to actually seek it out. We can be committed to discovering it. We can seek to suppress it. We can share it even when that would be inappropriate. We can also be indifferent to it.

In his *New York Times* bestseller *On Bullshit*, Harry Frankfurt differentiates lying from bullshitting. Both involve a departure from truth as our goal. One person may try to get things right but fail. Another person, the liar, may be trying to deceive their audiences into believing something that they know is false. But this is importantly different from the bullshitter, whose intention isn't either to promote the true or the false. For the liar, the difference between the true and the false is important. The bullshitter, however, isn't focused on whether what they're saying is true or not. The bullshitter instead bluffs or fakes a concern for the truth. Frankfurt considers an anecdote from Fania Pascal. Pascal had just had her tonsils out when Ludwig Wittgenstein called on her at a care facility. Pascal told him, 'I feel just like a dog that has been run over.' This description upset Wittgenstein, who apparently retorted, 'You don't know what a dog that has been run over feels like.' To most of us, it's pretty obvious that Pascal was simply using an expression. But Wittgenstein was upset because he took her claim to be one disconnected from any concern for how things really are:

> The point that troubles Wittgenstein is manifestly not that Pascal has made a mistake in her description of how she feels. Nor is it even that she has made a careless mistake…Her fault is not that she fails to get things right; but that she is not even trying.

And it is precisely this indifference to the truth that Frankfurt thinks is the essence of bullshit.

The intellectually honest person, then, will be the one who cares about the truth, both in its discovery and its sharing as appropriate. But truth is hard to find, and we shouldn't say that it's only the person who has found the truth who can be intellectually honest. We also care about honestly evaluating our own beliefs, and the reasons we have them, even if we can't be sure that those beliefs are true. And we need to be ready to acknowledge when we don't know things, or achieved certain goals only with the help of others. The intellectually honest person cares for the truth in disclosing both what is known and who really discovered it. The care for truth permeates their work.

Intellectual curiosity

In the *Theaetetus*, Plato's Socrates says that the feeling of wonder 'is very characteristic of a philosopher', that is, of a lover of wisdom. Indeed, says Socrates, 'philosophy has no other starting-point' than wonder. The Greek word here, $\theta\alpha\upsilon\mu\acute{\alpha}\zeta\epsilon\iota\nu$, is translated not only as wonder, but also as puzzlement. Picking up on this theme, Aristotle also connected philosophy with wonder:

> It is through wonder that [people] now begin and originally began
> to philosophize; wondering in the first place at obvious perplexities,
> and then by gradual progression raising questions about the greater
> matters too, e.g. about the changes of the moon and of the sun,
> about the stars and about the origin of the universe.

The person who wonders is struck by 'obvious perplexities' and is bothered by them. The person who wonders about some topic and is perplexed by it 'feels that he is ignorant' and thus has a reason to try to figure out what they're ignorant of. They possess a certain sort of inquisitiveness. Or, we might say, they exhibit intellectual curiosity or inquisitiveness.

But we need to be careful; it may not be that all curiosity involves wonder or the love of wisdom. For there seem to be kinds of curiosity that aren't excellences; we need to differentiate virtuous forms of curiosity from vicious forms. Websites known for click-bait titles prey on a kind of curiosity that doesn't contribute to our well-being. ('Do pineapples make great iPhone cases?' Unsurprisingly, the answer after a few clicks is 'no'.) Or consider gossip. Although some gossips take delight in having the information to share, others simply like to have it for themselves. Think, for instance, of those who regularly read *People*, *Star*, or *In Touch* in order to learn the latest celebrity gossip. Their desire fuels a multi-billion-dollar industry that pays for invasive photographs of famous people—and their children. Unbridled curiosity that serves no good purpose is bad for ourselves, as well as our relationship to those around us. Properly calibrated curiosity is a kind of deeply rooted care for important and valuable epistemic goals, such as knowledge, that move a person to inquiry in such a way as to achieve these goals. And the kinds of curiosity that feed our vacuous desires for trite information or delight in gossip are not rooted in this kind of virtuous care.

Intellectual open-mindedness

In his provocative Kenyon College commencement address, later published under the title 'This is Water', David Foster Wallace tells the story of two men talking in a bar in the Alaskan wilderness:

> One of the guys is religious, the other is an atheist, and they're arguing about the existence of God with that special intensity that comes after about the fourth beer. And the atheist says: 'Look, it's not like I don't have actual reasons for not believing in God. It's not like I haven't ever experimented with the whole God-and-prayer thing. Just last month I got caught away from the camp in that terrible blizzard, and I was totally lost and I couldn't see a thing, and it was fifty below, and so I did, I tried it: I fell to my knees in

the snow and cried out, "God, if there is a God, I'm lost in this blizzard, and I'm gonna die if you don't help me'".

And now, in the bar, the religious guy looks at the atheist all puzzled: 'Well then, you must believe now', he says. 'After all, here you are, alive'.

The atheist just rolls his eyes like the religious guy is a total simp: 'No, man, all that happened was that a couple Eskimos happened to come wandering by, and they showed me the way back to camp'.

One lesson this story illustrates, Wallace claims, is to note that the same experience can mean different things to different people given their different beliefs and ways of seeing the world. A second lesson is that given this fact about how we come to have our beliefs, we also have to be careful to not hold on to our beliefs too tightly. Two different people can experience the same thing in different ways. We need to take pains to avoid 'arrogance, blind certainty, a closed-mindedness that's like an imprisonment so complete that the prisoner doesn't even know he's locked up'. There's a strong human disposition to believe what we want to believe. And when we believe something simply because we want it to be true and believe it because we want to believe it, rather than because we have good reason to believe it, we're engaged in self-deception.

Part of avoiding self-deception is the need to be open-minded. Open-minded people are willing to listen to differing opinions and follow the evidence where it leads, even if they initially have opposing views they're strongly committed to. The truth, or the responsible pursuit of it, matters more than their need 'to be right'. The more a belief matters to us, the more reason we have to engage in self-deception to protect that belief.

One way of being self-deceived is via the Dunning–Kruger effect, a cognitive bias whereby people falsely overestimate their intellectual skill. In one study, 90 per cent of drivers indicated that they were above-average drivers. As the two psychologists, Kruger and Dunning, put it in their influential paper, 'people who lack the knowledge or wisdom to perform well are often unaware of this fact...The very same incompetence that leads them to make wrong choices also deprives them of the savvy necessary to recognize competence, be it their own or anyone else's.' Among those people who think that they're above-average drivers will be some who are unaware of the ways that their driving does not live up to that standard.

Intellectual courage and perseverance

Part of being open-minded requires us to be willing to question our own beliefs, even—and perhaps especially—those that we hold very closely. Two other virtues—intellectual courage and perseverance—are closely related to open-mindedness, as well as to each other. We can think of intellectual courage as the disposition to resist or overcome obstacles or threats in the pursuit of intellectual goods, a tendency to continue to pursue the truth in the face of difficulties that induce fear. Similarly, let's take intellectual perseverance to be the disposition to put in the proper time and effort in the pursuit of intellectual goods, despite the obstacles that might stand in one's way in securing those goods.

Without intellectual courage with respect to our beliefs, open-mindedness might lead us to an intellectual wishy-washiness where our beliefs are unstable and subject to the whims of whatever evidence we've most recently encountered. But intellectual virtue doesn't require that our beliefs are ungrounded and need not lead us to a scepticism that we can't have true beliefs. It just involves a willingness to revise one's beliefs in light of new evidence or sensitivity to aspects of the evidence we already possess. But that willingness should be tempered by a commitment to those beliefs that have good evidence for them.

Intellectual courage can help us endure the hardship of seeking the truth or other epistemic goods, pursuing it as best we can. But it can also help us 'stick to our intellectual convictions' once we have those beliefs. So long as our beliefs are well founded, the self-confidence that intellectual courage leads to shouldn't be seen as arrogance or hubris. Even if others mock us or threaten us for our beliefs, intellectual courage helps us stand up for them. Just as Malala's courage helped her stand up to the threat of the Taliban, so too her intellectual courage helped her stand up against the cultural pressure to believe that girls shouldn't be educated.

Margaret Ann Bulkley displayed intellectual perseverance. Born in Ireland at the end of the 18th century, Bulkley knew that women had fewer career options. When her uncle died and left her with a little money, Margaret used her inheritance to enroll, in 1809, in the University of Edinburgh's medical school. But the university didn't allow women to enrol, and so Bulkley disguised herself as a man—James Barry—to study medicine. Bulkley, still disguised as James Barry, then joined the British Army as a medic and worked her way up to become the chief medical inspector in Britain's Cape Colony. This story indicates not only the ability to resist the threat of being found out, but also a commitment to the time and energy it takes to train as a doctor in light of that threat.

Intellectual charity

None of us likes to be wrong. And we don't like those groups that we align ourselves with to be wrong either. So, we not only need to take care that we evaluate our own beliefs carefully and with an open mind to avoid self-deception, we also need to make sure that we evaluate others' ideas with a good standard. We want to give them the benefit of the doubt that we'd like others to give to our own ideas.

Intellectual charity requires that we not present ideas in ways that misrepresent or otherwise undermine them. Consider the debate in the early 2010s about the Affordable Care Act in the United States. Republican political strategists knew that their

Table 1 CNBC poll: Obamacare

very positive	14%
somewhat positive	15%
neutral	13%
somewhat negative	11%
very negative	35%
don't know/not sure	12%

constituents were less likely to support the bill if it was aligned with then-President Barack Obama, a Democrat. So they began referring to the bill not by its actual name, but as 'Obamacare'. And various polls showed that people responded differently to the bill depending on what it was called. One 2013 poll, run by CNBC news, found that 'Obamacare' was more polarizing than 'the Affordable Care Act', despite being the very same legislation. Table 1 shows the reported feelings when asked about Obamacare. And Table 2 shows the results when the very same question was asked about the Affordable Care Act:

Table 2 CNBC poll: Affordable Care Act

very positive	10%
somewhat positive	12%
neutral	11%
somewhat negative	13%
very negative	24%
don't know/not sure	30%

Unsurprisingly, the change in terminology affected people's political affiliation. When the data were broken down by political party, the poll found that Republicans viewed the bill more negatively when it was referred to as Obamacare, with Democrats viewing it more positively when referred to this way.

These results suggest that people's opinions on the bill were shaped not just by the contents of the bill, but how they saw the bill relating to their own political party. Not exactly the model of intellectual excellence.

We ought, therefore, to evaluate ideas in their best possible light, doing our best to accurately understand them before evaluating them, lest our biases colour how we evaluate them. If there's uncertainty about exactly what those ideas are, we ought to interpret them charitably. (Given that this virtue involves treating those with whom we disagree fairly, we could also refer to it as intellectual fairness.) Nicholas Wolterstorff puts the principle of charity this way: 'Thou must not take cheap shots. Thou must not sit in judgement until thou hast done thy best to understand. Thou must earn the right to disagree.' But intellectual charity involves how we evaluate our own positions as well. Wolterstorff continues: 'Genuine engagement entails both an effort to internalize the arguments of opposing viewpoints, understanding them from the inside, and an effort to examine one's own position from the outside, testing it for weaknesses.'

If our goal is truth, we ought to approach even the arguments of our so-called 'opponents' in a cooperative spirit, seeking to discover what we can learn from them, rather than being guided by a combative spirit. Debate should be done cooperatively rather than competitively.

This discussion of intellectual virtue hasn't sought to be exhaustive. There are a range of other epistemic excellences that we haven't addressed. There is, for example, the excellence of knowing those topics of inquiry that are most deserving of our inquiry. We haven't discussed intellectual vigilance or generosity. We haven't focused on those intellectual virtues that are inherently social in nature, such as trust or *eubulia* (the virtue of knowing from whom we should take counsel). The whole range of intellectual virtues are excellences that make us better thinkers and believers.

We can think of epistemic vices as those dispositions to feel, to think, and to behave in ways that are epistemically harmful. The vice of epistemic complacency is just one example. Epistemic vices can harm us not just individually but also corporately; that is, they can harm us politically. Quassim Cassam uses the 2003 US-led invasion of Iraq, and the search for alleged weapons of mass destruction, to illustrate the vice of closed-mindedness. Senior military figures, including army chief of staff General Eric Shinseki, told the Bush administration that at least 300,000 troops would be needed to pacify Iraq. President Bush, on the advice of Defense Secretary Rumsfeld, thought that 40,000 troops would be sufficient. (About 130,000 US troops ended up being sent.) A Pulitzer Prize-winning journalist described the Bush administration's approach to the invasion of Iraq as 'arrogant' and 'impervious to evidence'. Our epistemic practices have real-world consequences.

Chapter 4
Islamic and Confucian accounts of the virtues

Virtues East and West

Reflection on the virtues has played a key role in Western philosophy dating back to the ancient Greek philosophers. It also plays an important role in Christianity, in part because many Christian theologians sought to incorporate what they took to be insights from the Greek and Roman intellectual traditions. But this doesn't mean that these two parts of the virtue tradition have the exact same view of the virtues in mind. Aristotle, for instance, thought that the '*megalopsychos*'—literally the 'great-souled' person—was the paragon of virtue. He thought the *megalopsychos* was 'worthy of the greatest things' and was 'the best person'. The great-souled person also recognizes that they are worthy of great things. And since the great-souled person is accurate in their own moral evaluation, they really are worthy of great honours. But Aristotle thought that this individual would be ashamed to receive goods from others, since he also thought it inferior to receive goods from another rather than to do them oneself. Since the *megalopsychos* seeks to be morally superior, they don't want to be dependent on others. The *megalopsychos* values self-reliance since receiving goods from others would appear to threaten their own excellence.

Others in the virtue tradition think that this kind of self-reliance ought not be aspired to, either because it simply fails to understand the communal nature of human dependency or because it fails to recognize that dependency on others need not detract from our excellence. Christian theologians, for instance, would reject that any human is capable of moral goodness without reliance on others. Thinking otherwise, for the Christian, involves a kind of naive hubris. Those communities that approach virtue along Aristotelian lines will honour the great-souled individual. But other communities, oriented toward other pictures of what the virtues are and require, won't.

We see then that even across traditions that stress the virtues, there isn't always agreement about what the correct list of virtues is. The commitment to the importance of the virtues as moral excellences doesn't, by itself, tell us what those virtues are. The primary purpose of this chapter is to see how two different cultural traditions understand virtue, namely Islam and Confucianism. Like people in all cultures, agents in these traditions acquire and exercise the virtues as accommodated to their own specific cultural and religious contexts that elevate some specific virtues above others; the difference here is that these cultures diverge significantly from other notions of what virtues operate within a larger social and religious context. These traditions demonstrate that one's understanding of particular virtues, and even what qualities constitute virtues, depends on the cultural and theoretic context in which they develop.

Virtue in Islam

Virtue plays an important role in the Islamic faith. The Arabic word for 'Islam' itself means 'submission' or 'surrender', specifically submission to Allah (God). Followers of Islam are called Muslims, an Arabic word that refers to 'those who submit to God'. Muslims believe that Muhammad wrote the Qur'ān, an oral revelation from

Allah given through the angel Gabriel. As the very word of Allah, it is authoritative for all Muslims. Verses in the Qur'ān demand that Muslims be just, moderate, and charitable. But, as with other religions such as Christianity or Judaism, there's not a single agreed-upon understanding of what Islamic belief requires. A number of different divisions have developed. For instance, Sunni and Shia Muslims differ on which of Muhammad's successors were legitimate and, as a result, who can be a subsequent *imam*. Mu'tazilite theology is an especially rationalistic school which holds that human reason, including that found in Greek philosophy such as Aristotle, can be a source of knowledge. One noticeable Mu'tazilite Muslim was Al-Kindi (9th century CE), who sought to make Greek philosophy as a whole unified and show it to be consistent with the Qur'ān. In contrast, Ash'ārite theology, the largest school of Sunni Islam, is more traditionalist. Certain things are good or required simply because they are commanded by God. In fact, it is God's commanding them that makes them good.

Obedience to the commands of Allah serves as the starting point for all the virtues and how later thinkers develop these qualities. The key question then is 'What does God require of me?' In one sense, the answer to this question is given by the five pillars of Islam since these are obligatory for all Muslims. The first of these, the *shahadah*, is the central Islamic profession of faith: 'there is no god but Allah and Muhammad is his prophet'. The second pillar, *salat*, is ritual prayers that are to be offered, prostrate, five times a day in the direction of Mecca. These prayers are a theological practice that orients, literally, every Muslim every day. *Zakat*, the third pillar, is sometimes referred to as 'the poor rate' and involves giving a fixed portion of one's wealth to those in need as an act of almsgiving. The fourth pillar, *sawm*, requires Muslims to fast from food, drink, sex, and smoking sunrise to sunset during the holy month of Ramadan. The last pillar is the *hajj*, a pilgrimage to Mecca that is required of all those who can make it at least once during their lifetime.

These five pillars, however, should not be seen just as required behaviours. Their purpose is to foster proper inner dispositions. The purpose of *salat*, for example, is to focus one's mind and inner life on Allah. *Zakat* requires not just giving of money, but that it be done out of a spirit of generosity and compassion for those in need, purifying oneself from miserliness. One should pray prostrate to reinforce a spirit of humility. In living out the five pillars, one becomes a person properly related to Allah and to others. In this context, *adab* (the manner in which people acquire good character) provides an entrée into Islamic accounts of the virtues. Muhammad said that 'The most perfect of you in faith is the one who attains excellence in character and is most kind to his kin.'

His later followers, most notably Ibn Mishkawayh (932–1030 CE), Ibn Sina (980–1037 CE), and Al-Ghazzali (1058–1111 CE), often engaged the Aristotelian virtues within the larger context of Islamic theology. The virtues of generosity, justice, and wisdom emerged as central character traits—but in the thinkers after Ibn Sina and Ibn Mishkawayh the virtues themselves took a more religious turn as theologians made a concerted effort to understand and implement the teachings of the Qur'ān and the Sunnah (the traditions and practices of the prophet Muhammad). Obedience and justice are closely related since justice (at least on the part of the human person) requires obedience to the Creator. Justice concerns giving to God what is owed but it is also one of the most important divine attributes; and God, therefore, demands that we demonstrate it to our fellow human beings. Justice requires that we practise fairness in all our dealings with others regardless of their social standing. We are to cultivate qualities where we do not exploit the helpless, practise faithfulness in promise-keeping, and develop an honest character. Generosity, like justice, also reflects God's nature in that Allah is merciful, charitable, and gracious; so we too are to be charitable, merciful, and gracious to others. But it is wisdom that enables us to determine—often in terms of a 'mean' as borrowed from Aristotle,

given the influence of Aristotle on many in the Islamic tradition—
how we should practise justice and generosity. Yet, in each of these
virtues, the Islamic tradition of the virtues demonstrates a
distinctly religious orientation of the self towards God.

The work of Al-Ghazzali, sometimes described as the most
important Muslim after Muhammad, gives us insight into the
central role of virtue for Islam (Figure 6). Al-Ghazzali was a
member of the Ash'ārite school. As a teacher at one of the leading
theological schools in Baghdad, Al-Ghazzali was critical of the
influence of Neoplatonic philosophy on other Muslims. These
criticisms are developed in his book *The Incoherence of the
Philosophers*. His best-known work is *The Revival of the Religious
Sciences (Ihya'ul ulumuddin)*, a nearly-2,400-page work in Arabic
on Islamic practice. Al-Ghazzali also wrote a Persian summary of
The Revival entitled *The Alchemy of Happiness (Kimyāyé
Sa'ādat)*. *The Alchemy*, like the earlier *Revival* on which it's based,
is a manual for spiritual formation. Since, as is also the case in
Christian Europe during the same period, there was no clear line
between medieval Islamic theology and philosophy (*falasifa*),
spiritual formation includes ethics which for Al-Ghazzali is based
on the cultivation and practice of virtue. In the *Alchemy*, he seeks
to show how to transform a base and vicious soul into a virtuous
soul, just as alchemy sought to transform a base metal into a
valuable metal using the 'philosopher's stone'. By developing
virtues we draw close to Allah, bringing about our 'spiritual
happiness' (*sa'ādat*).

Toward this goal, the book is divided into four sections, called
pillars. The first pillar is 'Acts of Worship', and describes the kind
of religious behaviour, such as *shahadah*, *salat*, and the ritual
purification, that following Allah requires. But, as indicated above,
this should not be understood to just require external actions or
prohibitions, but also the right inner orientation in doing them.
Submission to Allah requires that we perfect our inner character.
The second pillar is 'Mutual Relations', describing rules that

The Virtues

6. A Persian manuscript of Al-Ghazzali's *Alchemy of Happiness* where he describes the process of transformation from vice to virtue.

should govern social interactions such as marriage and trade. The centrality of virtue for the *Alchemy* is most evident in the last two pillars. The section titled 'The Destroyers' lists barriers or veils to virtue—namely various vices such as greed, haughtiness, frivolousness, miserliness, hypocrisy, hatred, and self-conceit. The last section, 'The Deliverers', addresses how to overcome those obstacles that stand in the way of our happiness by developing virtues such as hope, poverty (understood as contentment with few material possessions), asceticism, and sincerity.

Al-Ghazzali refers to the *Alchemy* as a work in 'psychology', but this should be understood in the broader sense of a science of the whole human person or soul (in Greek, *psyche*) rather than the more restricted discipline of modern psychology. Psychology, for Al-Ghazzali, includes the whole of our relationship to God, others, and ourselves. These relationships are interconnected given that God is a unity and creates and sustains the entire universe.

> Know that there is a station in spiritual insight where, when a person reaches it, he really sees that all that exists is interconnected, one with another, and all are like one animate being. The relationship of the parts of the world, such as the heavens, the earth, the stars to each other, is like the relationship of the parts of one animate being to each other.

It is Islam's monotheism (*hitmat al-'amalī*) that forms the unity of all knowledge and understanding.

The process of becoming a good person begins with knowledge. According to Muhammad, 'the quest for knowledge is incumbent upon every Muslim'. We come to know more about Allah by knowing ourselves and our dependence upon Allah: 'Know thyself and thou knowest thy Lord.' Knowledge of what we should be like isn't enough for us to develop the character we know we ought to. Reason is only a guide, not a master. But we're internally divided. Al-Ghazzali refers to the moral life as a struggle between competing armies inside us. We have to force ourselves to develop the virtues—to train the good army—through exercise of our free will (or will power) informed by reason. Al-Ghazzali refers to this process as 'the greater struggle' (*jihād al-akbar*). Once we become virtuous, our external actions will be pleasing to Allah since they are expressions of our inner commitments and qualities.

It is here that virtue is central to Al-Ghazzali's thought. States are dispositions of character that can be either positive or negative.

> The power of anger, should it become excessive, is called impetuosity; while if it is deficient, it is called cowardice and spiritlessness. When it is in balance—not too much or too little—it is called courage. Courage gives rise to nobility, high-mindedness, bravery, mildness, patience, moderation, control of anger, and characteristics like these. From impetuosity come boasting, vanity, conceit, recklessness, vainglory, throwing oneself into dangerous affairs, and the like. From its deficiency come self-abasement, helplessness, fawning, and abjectness.

Our desires and emotions motivate us toward action. But not all motivation directs us toward our ultimate good. Al-Ghazzali describes our emotions as stubborn animals that need to be tamed.

Similarly, through habituation, we can come to train our desires and emotions. For example, by engaging in *sawm* during Ramadan, we gradually habituate our desire for food away from what is bad for us:

> Know that the object of hunger is the breaking of the self, bringing it under control, and correcting it...The object is not pain and hunger. Rather, the object is that one eat that amount which neither makes his stomach heavy nor leaves the feeling of hunger. Both of these distract one from worship.

Our happiness thus requires that we triumph over our carnal appetites and develop virtue. Specific virtues that we need to develop include zeal, patience, sincerity, commitment, courage, temperance, and wisdom. When we develop the virtues, we achieve the happiness that Al-Ghazzali describes as 'the angelic state' and 'eternal happiness'.

Given his reliance on Aristotle, Al-Ghazzali's account of the virtues shares many similarities with those in the Christian tradition. But the exact details of what those virtues are like and how they relate to religious practice differ for Al-Ghazzali from philosophers in the Christian tradition. We find an even more divergent approach in traditional Confucian philosophy.

Virtue in Confucianism

The Confucian tradition embraces not only the work of Confucius (555–479 BCE; also known as Kongzi), but also that of subsequent thinkers. Of these Mencius (372–289 BCE; also known as Mengzi) and Xunzi (3rd century BCE) are the best known. While there are important differences between the thinkers in the Confucian tradition, some of which are discussed below, they all emphasized the *dao* (the 'way') as providing the highest human good and the proper cosmic ordering of the universe. The *dao* gives us guidance on how to live a harmonious life and structure our society. The morally wise and good or exemplary person (the *jungzi*) follows and promotes the *dao*.

Confucius' teachings were compiled and edited by his disciples in the *Analects*, a collection of short, aphoristic sayings attributed to 'the Master' rather than an extended and systematic treatise on virtue. For instance, 'The Master said, "Exemplary persons [*junzi*] cherish their excellence; petty persons cherish their land. Exemplary persons cherish fairness; petty persons cherish the thought of gain."' These sayings are clearly intended to guide our behaviour and feelings, even if they don't give a fully worked out ethical theory. Nevertheless, Confucius understood the *dao* as giving us a unified and holistic vision of how to live.

For Confucius, the well-lived human life is one that aligns with the *dao*. The *dao* could be found in the Zhou dynasty (approximately the 18th to 12th centuries BCE). But by his time, Confucius thought, the *dao* had been lost. What was needed was a return to the golden era of the Zhou, which he understood as a model society. With the decline of the Zhou dynasty and its replacement with feudal lords and warring factions, 'the world has long been without the *dao*'. Confucius sought to rediscover lost teachings and traditions, reinstating them, rather than inaugurating a new way forward: 'I transmit and do not create.' Restoring the *dao* was, for Confucius, a divinely commanded task. And completing this task required a return to the wisdom embedded in earlier Chinese traditions. Rediscovering earlier religious rituals and customs (*li*) helps us live the *dao*, for the good life is a life of doing, cultivating the heart and mind, rather than just learning doctrine.

Confucius asked, 'Where is the human *dao*?' Recapturing the *dao* requires bringing people back to the correct path by cultivating *de*, a dispositional character that is often translated as 'virtue'. *De*, here, is the manifestation of the *dao* in a virtuous life: 'I set my heart on *dao*, and base myself on *de*.' Cultivation of virtuous *de* should be our highest concern, but it's not an easy task. It requires behaving well in our interactions with others, feeling what we ought to feel, and fulfilling our religious obligations. Not only is shaping our own character difficult, but Confucius also insisted that the *dao* shouldn't be understood in just an individualistic way.

The *dao* provides a model for how a family should be structured, with different members having different roles in the flourishing of the family as a whole. The family unit is the most basic social unit, and the one where our bonds with others are first formed. Familial and kinship relations are often understood hierarchically, such as between a parent and a child or an older sibling and a younger. Since the family provides the paradigm for larger social groups, our obligations to others can be seen as extensions of the kinds of obligations we have toward family members and are thus also asymmetric. For instance, the respect and obedience due a ruler is modelled on *xiao*, which is the respect and piety due one's parents, elders, and ancestors. The relationships involved in *xiao* are asymmetric. Children owe their parents deference; but parents owe their children care. This understanding of filial piety in turn provides the framework for understanding other relationships. *Di*, or brotherly piety, focuses on the love and respect owed to older siblings by younger. The further one expands beyond the family in concentric circles, the less strong these obligations are. But they never fully dissipate. The family unit thus also serves as the foundation for all our social obligations. Confucius describes *xiao* and the respect due an older brother as 'the root of complete goodness'.

Society is an extension of the family unity writ large. In this way, Confucianism involves an inherently communal view of virtue. Both the family and society as a whole seek to promote the good of all through hierarchy and division of obligations and roles, similar in some ways to how Plato thinks of the ideal city (*kallipolis*). This pattern found in the harmonious family is further extended in *ren*, where one's familial love is extended, though to a lesser degree, to all of one's community and ultimately to all of humanity. Another central Confucian text, *The Great Learning*, records Confucius saying that the development of *ren* is good not just for the family, but also for social and political communities in general: 'when the personal life is cultivated, the family will be regulated; when the family is regulated, the state will be in order; and when the state is in order, there will be peace throughout the world.'

The *jungzi* is the 'exemplary person'—one who possesses virtue in its most complete way by practising *ren*. The virtue of *ren*—which the *jungzi* learns at an early age in the home—helps to guide and shape the other virtues as a kind of master virtue or principle of complete integration. Specifically, *ren* refers to benevolence or care that the Master describes as 'loving all men'. However, it also has a broader meaning that includes the other virtues. The other key virtues that the *jungzi* possesses include *xiao* (piety), *yi* (righteousness), *li* (ritual propriety), *zhi* (wisdom), and *xin* (trustworthiness). *Ren*, particularly when understood as the specific virtue governing the care a ruler has for those under their charge, is balanced by *yi*, the virtue governing the appropriate obedience and conformity that those in a community have for their ruler.

Yi is a kind of justice or righteousness that enables its possessor to do the right thing—or that which is fitting—given the context. *Yi* is often translated as 'righteousness' or 'appropriateness', though it also involves elements often associated with justice. *Yi* involves the ability to recognize and balance competing obligations that pull one in different directions. Developing *yi* allows us to fulfil our various roles and obligations in an overall harmonious way. And one can't have *yi* without being properly oriented toward other virtues such as truthfulness and courage. *Li* expresses the kinds of propriety in the relationships a person has with reference to his religious obligations, the parent–child relationship, and discharging these responsibilities with the proper respect. *Zhi* is the ability to know and choose the right thing to do in a multiplicity of situations and contexts while *xin* is the quality of trustworthiness. These virtues—as in the tradition of Aristotle—reflect the primacy of the social order—with particular attention to the Chinese tradition of piety and integrity—and a person's appropriate practices within it. Role responsibilities are meant to provide meaning and structure, rather than be restrictive.

The virtues, in Confucian thought, shouldn't just be seen as governing external behaviour. Actions need to be motivated by the right concern and done with the appropriate accompanying feeling. So becoming a *jungzi* involves training how we see the world and having the right attitude of 'sympathetic concern' (*shu*) and respect. In the *Analects* Confucius writes that 'nowadays, those who provide [for their parents] are called filial. However, even dogs and horses are given provisions. If there is no reverence—what is the difference'? What matters for the *dao* isn't just our actions—even animals do good actions—but also the spirit or character that those actions flow from (Figure 7).

Subsequent Confucian thinkers like Mencius and Xunzi would depart from Confucius' teachings in a number of ways, showing that Confucianism too is a tradition and not a monolith. Perhaps the most famous of these departures shows up in the Confucian debates about human nature. Confucianism in general holds that both the *dao* and happiness require the fulfilment of *xing* (nature

7. **Confucius handing on the collective wisdom of *ren* to his disciples, who show due respect for their teacher.**

or human nature). Virtue makes one a true human being. As a result, the *jungzi* are the most genuinely human. But there is disagreement about how to understand *xing*. Confucius didn't elaborate his view of human nature, a point of frustration for his disciples. In the *Analects* we read 'What the Master has to say about human nature and the way of Heaven we cannot get to hear.' It seems likely that he thought it was neutral. By contrast, Mencius thought that *xing* is inherently good; and Xunzi held it to be bad or skewed towards vices. Mencius thought that all people contained in them 'sprouts' (*duan*) of virtue, as evidenced by our characteristic tendency to care for other humans.

> The heart and mind of compassion is the sprout of benevolence, the heart and mind of shame is the sprout of righteousness, the heart and mind of complaisance is the sprout of propriety, and the heart and mind of judging right and wrong is the sprout of knowledge. Human beings have these four sprouts just as they have four limbs.

Since human nature is thus oriented to what is good for us, we don't need to fundamentally reject our natural inclinations. We just have to nurture and grow them, as one might nurture and grow rice. But without proper cultivation the sprouts will wither, just as uncared for rice will wither or drown in a rice paddy. Such botanical metaphors play a central role in Mencius' thought. By learning from and following the sages, all humans could follow the proper course of development and become *jungzi*. Mencius held that human viciousness was exclusively a function of failing to follow the *dao*. Since most humans fail to follow the way, this shows that absent proper cultivation and care most humans are evil by nature. Mengzi also thought that virtuous development could only take place in a nurturing environment. Vicious communities, like a rice paddy with too little water, will produce a bad crop.

The Doctrine of the Mean, one of the four central texts of Confucian philosophy, was written by Confucius' grandson, Zisi.

In the *Analects*, Confucius is recorded as saying that 'virtue embodied in the doctrine of the mean is of the highest order'. But what exactly this doctrine involves isn't indicated. Zisi seeks to flesh this out in *The Doctrine of the Mean*, showing how to develop a balance or harmony. One finds here, much like in Aristotle but developed independently, that one should never act or feel in excess: 'the superior man embodies the course of the mean'. The course of the mean requires proper self-evaluation or self-watchfulness. It also requires leniency and toleration in our interactions with others. What is appropriate for interactions depends upon the social relationship in question. It wouldn't be appropriate, for instance, for rulers to treat their ministers in the same way that ministers treat their rulers; nor would it be appropriate for fathers to serve their sons in the way that sons should serve their fathers. The course of the mean also requires that we fully develop our human natures and equip others to do the same so that together we may 'assist the transforming and nourishing power of Heaven and Earth'.

The point of this discussion isn't to give a full Confucian, and thus Eastern, way of understanding virtue. And it's certainly not to try and fit Confucian approaches to virtue into categories from the Western philosophical tradition. Confucian views deserve to be understood on their own terms. Confucian thought can only be forced into a Western approach to virtue at the cost of the larger patterns of thought and culture in which it developed. But seeing how virtue plays a central role in ethical traditions ranging from ancient Greece to medieval Islam to ancient and contemporary Chinese thought illustrates how broad the cultural impact of the virtues has been, and is. Neo-Confucianism, a later development of Confucianism from its encounter with Buddhism and Taoism, continues to be influential in China, Korea, Japan, and Vietnam. The breadth of reflection on the virtues also demonstrates how different cultures shape the exact understanding of the virtues. While virtues are central to Western philosophy and religion, we see that their importance can be found in other traditions as well.

The lists of virtues are shaped by the cultures in which they're developed and therefore are accommodated to their own specific cultural and religious contexts that elevate some specific virtues above others. But despite these differences, the virtues still play a central role in how to understand perfected individuals and their roles in society.

Chapter 5

The theological virtues: be good, by God!

Philosophical and theological accounts of the virtues

Although people of faith affirm values such as wisdom, justice, and courage, they also frequently emphasize other character traits that seem to be especially religious in nature. Examples include forgiveness, grace, obedience, charity, and faith. So why, in addition to these 'secular' virtues, do religious people feel a need to add their own? Are they articulating a more complete sense of what it means to be a good person?

Historically, there has been significant overlap between religious and secular accounts of the virtues. But where the ancient Greek philosophers saw their virtues as fairly complete lists, Muslim, Jewish, and Christian thinkers saw those lists from Greek thinkers as helpful but incomplete, offering starting points but in need of revisions to their definitions. In this chapter we focus on the theological virtues as initially presented in the Jewish tradition and then developed and augmented by later Christian thinkers. One way of thinking about these differences is to contrast the way in which non-theists (that is, those who don't believe God exists) and theists (those who do believe that God exists) consider the good. For Aristotle, a virtue was simply a good habit of the soul that facilitated our development for the sake of the good. For a religious person, a virtue might be understood as 'being good for God'. Aquinas appeals to the medieval theologians' standard summary of Augustine's definition when he writes, 'virtue is a good quality of the mind, by which we live righteously, of which no one can make bad use, which God works in us, without us'. That is, a virtue is a good quality of the soul that enables us to act well. Moreover, it is ultimately God who enables us to act for the good. This last point is important since for those in theistic traditions of the virtues, there is always a theocentric understanding of those good qualities God desires for us and helps us achieve.

Jewish and Christian origins of the theological virtues

The Jewish Scriptures consistently emphasized the idea of 'righteousness' within the context of the covenant God established with Abraham and his descendants. Faithfulness to the covenant was a key element of righteousness, but so too was the acquisition of other important character traits such as gratitude, mercy, and humility. The authors of the wisdom literature (e.g. Proverbs, Ecclesiastes, Psalms, Job) repeatedly told their hearers to 'get wisdom'. The prophets (e.g. Isaiah, Jeremiah, Amos, and Micah) often spoke of a righteousness that practised compassion. The prophet Micah, for example, exhorted his listeners to 'love justice, show mercy, and walk humbly' with God.

In the Pentateuch (the first five books of the Hebrew Bible), the authors place a good deal of emphasis upon keeping various laws which range from what we can call 'moral precepts' (such as 'Do not murder' and 'Honour your father and mother') to various kinds of dietary or 'ceremonial precepts' (such as 'Do not eat shellfish' and 'Do not touch the skin of a pig'). But moving into the prophetic books more emphasis is placed upon the inner dispositions of people rather than just a list of external actions to do or avoid.

The prophets focused on a righteousness that was not merely a personal piety towards God but also a social obligation to others. These twin obligations to God and others were based upon God's gracious activity in establishing a covenant with Abraham—and God's promise to bless those who kept the covenant. The prophet Isaiah touches on the importance of not merely assenting to the precepts of the covenant but also having them shape one's life in a substantial way. Speaking on behalf of God, he says, 'These people draw near with their mouths and honour me with their lips, while their hearts are far from me, and their worship of me is a human commandment learned by rote.' This passage contrasts two approaches to following God: that of merely 'following rules' and a more faithful approach that shapes the inward disposition of a person's heart. The inner disposition—the condition of one's heart—describes in phenomenological language the attitudes of both good and evil people. The good have an inner disposition to be kind, practise justice, and think humbly of themselves. In contrast, evil people—regardless of their outward behaviour—can harbour contempt, anger, and envy.

The passage also shows the inadequacy of simply 'following the rules'. On occasion it may be that justice requires violating a rule in order to treat others with respect or to attend to someone in need. For example, there may be a rule against violating the Sabbath, but a greater obligation may be to help another person in dire need. Thirteenth-century Rabbi Moses Maimonides considers the tensions between the rules of justice and the good of our neighbour in this way: 'The reason of a commandment, whether positive or negative, is clear, and its usefulness evident, if it directly tends to remove injustice, or to teach good conduct that furthers the well-being of society, or to impart a truth which ought to be believed either on its own merit or as being indispensable for facilitating the removal of injustice or the teaching of good morals.' There is a priority to the cultivation of justice as an inner disposition since the application of an external rule often fails in complex circumstances. And this is so because the care and well-being of persons serves as the orientation for the virtue of justice.

The Christian tradition sees itself in terms of a continuity with this Jewish emphasis on the heart and incorporates it into its own account of the teachings of Christ. In Matthew's Gospel, Christ is confronted by those who insist on an outward display of piety, for example in keeping the Sabbath. But he says, 'The sabbath was made for humanity, not humanity for the sabbath.' This person-centred approach to his teaching reaches a high point in the Beatitudes (the first section of Jesus's Sermon on the Mount) where he claims that blessedness, or happiness, comes to those who practise peace-making, who are merciful, who hunger and thirst for righteousness, and who have a pure heart—that is, the inward disposition to desire righteousness. Again, the shift is away from strict rules and laws to the cultivation of inward dispositions to care for persons.

The Apostle Paul also favours the cultivation of character over meticulous rule-following. He lists such qualities as 'fruits of the Spirit' (and elsewhere 'gifts of the Spirit'). These qualities include 'love, joy, peace, patience, kindness ... gentleness, and self-control. Against such things there is no law.' The life devoted to God shapes a person's inward dispositions so that rule-following eventually becomes irrelevant because the motivation and acquisition of character supersedes a stringent adherence to moral rules or laws.

The early Christians—like their Jewish forebears—employed language that lent itself to later developments of the virtues and vices. However, neither group developed the kind of moral psychology (or virtue and vice terminology) that considered how a person could cultivate these virtues in an organized and developmental way. Rather, people were told to 'Do justice' or 'Love one another'. As Wayne Meeks argues, the early Christians often simply appealed to God as a moral exemplar and were told to 'Be like God' in terms of cultivating qualities like love, compassion, mercy, peace, and purity. The prophets, Jesus, and the apostles made these lists of good qualities and referenced the condition of one's mind and heart without integrating these various elements into an account of how the virtues and vices worked.

Nevertheless, their account of these qualities and their descriptions were easily understood in terms of Platonic and Aristotelian virtue language. This enabled early Christian thinkers to bridge the philosophical and theological domains. In so doing, Christians introduced 'new' virtues to the discussion. Although the ancient Greeks and Romans used the words faith, hope, and love, the philosophers of antiquity never thought of these as virtues in the ways that Christian theologians did. The Christian Scriptures seemed to emphasize qualities that at times ran counter to Greek and Roman values in their rejection of honour and magnanimity in favour of humility and love. Augustine and Aquinas represent two significant (and somewhat different) streams of thought concerning the relationship of pagan values to theology.

The nature of the theological virtues

In order to understand how the theological virtues came to be differentiated from the moral virtues we need to look at how the ultimate goal of the religious life transcends how the Greek philosophers conceived it. But this means that differences will also appear regarding their cause—or acquisition—in that the theological virtues require more than mere human effort.

For philosophers like Plato, Aristotle, and Cicero, the virtues aimed at both the individual's good and the common good. For these thinkers, good people were those who governed themselves well and contributed to the overall well-being of society. Cicero, for example, said that the four cardinal virtues directed us to that which is true (wisdom), the good organization of society (justice), the greatness of a noble spirit (courage), and personal moderation (temperance). By practising the moral virtues, a person could not only order their own lives well but could also contribute to the common good. However, the Christian account of the human good extended beyond the scope of both ordering one's soul in this present world and the good of the state. Rather, 'The Good', in a theological context, is a person—God. The goal of all human activity becomes communion with God. In the pursuit of God, a person's life would naturally be well ordered and the common good could be found in the overarching divine Goodness.

One of the first Christian thinkers to develop the Christian virtues and their relationship to the cardinal virtues of the Greeks and Romans was Augustine. His fundamental orientation to all matters moral and theological was that of *Fides quarens intellectum*—'faith seeking understanding'. For him, the starting point for all inquiry was the perspective of faith since pagan philosophy could be a dangerous competitor. He thought that the theological virtues needed to supplant and transform the moral virtues of the secular world. When left to themselves, even the finest of the Graeco-Roman virtues as presented by philosophers were nothing more than 'glittering vices'. Only a right apprehension of the true God could ever order us and our affections correctly.

For Augustine, when we attempt to live simply by the cardinal virtues of the Greeks or Romans, we have established a kind of human standard of virtue that does not fully conform to the true virtue that God has ordained for us. It is a kind of attempt to justify ourselves by a standard of our own making. Augustine saw two problems here: an epistemological problem and a moral problem. The epistemological problem is that we really cannot know true virtue apart from what God has revealed to us. If we cannot know true virtue, we cannot practise it. And the moral problem is that our pride puffs us up with regard to thinking we are truly great in terms of the moral virtues. But this, in his view, is arrogance.

Yet other Christian thinkers, like Aquinas, were more than willing to allow that the cardinal virtues were actually virtues—since they were found in both the Hebrew and Christian Scriptures. For Aquinas, 'the light of natural reason' was a kind of natural revelation God shared with all peoples and cultures. All people, regardless of their theological convictions, know that prudence, justice, courage, and self-control truly are virtues. But Aquinas thought they need 'perfection'. His orientation to the issue of the secular virtues was that of *Gratia non tollit naturam, sed perficit*—'grace does not destroy nature but perfects it'. The moral virtues are not alien to the theological virtues but were a kind of first step toward the ultimate destination.

The Greek virtues were good but insufficient for the ultimate end to which God designed human beings: eternal communion with God and others. And that communion starts in this temporal life. Being wise and being temperate, for example, were clearly necessary for a civil society, but God doesn't only want peaceful coexistence and personal self-control. He also wants dedication to the Kingdom of God and love for all peoples: family and friends as well as strangers and foes. But how do we acquire these virtues? After all, the moral virtues are cultivated simply by imitation, effort, and practice. Why is it that thinkers like Augustine and Aquinas both contend that 'something more' is needed? In order to understand why this is the case, we need to note the Christian doctrine of sin.

Humans were created by God in a state of 'original justice'—that is, without sin. But through some cosmic or personal failing—sin—all humans ultimately fall short of the good they should do. People are morally flawed. Although we can grasp moral truths (such as the basic principles of natural law like 'Do not murder', 'Pursue justice', and 'Honour your mother and father'), we cannot consistently act on them in ways that free us entirely from moral evil.

8. The three theological virtues are almost always depicted together, as theologians held that a person could not have one without the other two.

The solution to sin is divine grace. Grace involves God doing in and for us what we cannot do ourselves. By receiving in faith the goodness that (or rather Who) is God, people can participate in the life of God with God's help. This enables us to not only live peacefully with others in community but also to live a life characterized by faith, hope, and love. In addition to this orientation to God with the infusion of the theological virtues, we also have a new way of considering how the cardinal virtues can be acquired (Figure 8).

The theological virtues are infused by God into a person at conversion. It is this acceptance of divine grace that distinguishes these infused virtues from the acquired virtues. We acquire the moral virtues through habituation, and although the moral virtues are good, by themselves they do not ensure that we achieve our divinely appointed ends. The infused virtues do this since the reception of divine grace also alters the moral virtues—that is, infuses them—so that a person can also obtain and perfect the moral virtues by divine grace. We can see then that there are not just two kinds of virtues—cardinal and theological—but three: acquired moral virtues, infused theological virtues, and infused moral virtues. These infused cardinal virtues retain their names but change their ultimate orientation to God. Prudence, for example, as an infused moral virtue orients all our deliberation towards the love of God and neighbour, not merely to the good of self-control or peaceful coexistence. The outward activity may be the same as produced by acquired prudence, but the inner disposition is reoriented to a greater good.

There is a hierarchical relationship among the theological virtues. Faith is trust-based intellectual assent to revealed theological truths. Trust, both in truths and also in persons, allows people to hope and reach out for the goods revealed in faith. That is, faith is not merely about assent to specific religious truths but also about the reliability of the one who reveals those truths. Like faith, hope requires a trust in God and is the patient expectation—or habit—of waiting for the promised but 'not-yet' good that faith points to. But the fullness of the theological virtues is charity. In this virtue, a person is united with God and with others in a kind of 'divine friendship' that surpasses the boundaries of family, ethnicity, gender, and status, thereby enabling the possessor to love even their enemies.

Faith

The question of the definition of faith seems to have a priority before going any further. Not all trust of or reliance on others is the theological virtue of faith. Jim Jones, the infamous cult leader, for example, presided over the mass murder-suicide of over 900 people in French Guyana in 1978. Worried that US agents would descend upon him and his followers, Jones had his assistants mix sedatives and cyanide with powdered drink mix for his devotees. In an 'act of faith' they drank it and died. Jones appealed to the idea that their 'faith' should lead them to believe him and his message. But what Jones advocated was not really faith; it was a kind of delusional mania created in order to manipulate his gullible followers. That is, faith, considered as a virtue, should be distinguished from things like gullibility and superstition, on the one hand, and more positive dispositions like knowledge and opinion, on the other hand.

Faith is not mere naive superstition or gullibility. A person might be taken in once by someone who is deceptive. And it is difficult to see how faith could function as a sustained habit over time if it were merely superstition. Faith, rather, is a kind of trust in another person where the other proves to be trustworthy. But since faith is not simply a one-off act of belief, it should also be distinguished from other kinds of habitual states of mind, most notably opinion and knowledge.

Faith is not mere opinion. An opinion is a judgement a person makes based upon the kinds of evidence presented to them by others or by their own experiences. I may have the opinion that chocolate ice-cream tastes better than vanilla. Or I may have the opinion that one friend is more trustworthy than another—and that I should trust her advice rather than his. Over time, my opinion that my one friend offers better advice than another can become solidified. Opinions may often vary with taste, with our own subjective experiences, and with the judgements we make based on others' testimonies. We often contrast these opinions, though, with facts—or what we might call 'knowledge'.

Opinions can be wrong. But knowledge is factive—that is, what is known must be true. (We can, of course, think that we know something that's false. But if it's false, we don't really know it.) If we know something, we both assent to its truth and what we assent to really is true. But notice that knowledge need not involve trust. I may know that a complex mathematical problem is true not because I trust someone else in giving me the answer, but because I'm good at differential equations.

80

Since knowledge isn't the same as faith, a person might know that God exists and yet not have faith. They might know *that* there is God and yet not know *who* God is. Faith has a kind of priority over knowledge about God in the life of the Christian for two reasons. First, a person needs to believe *in* God rather than just believe things *about* God in order to follow the teachings of the faith. Second, faith requires a relationship of trust in God. Aquinas writes that 'faith is a habit of the mind, whereby eternal life is begun in us, making the intellect assent to what is non-apparent'. And since we cannot possess knowledge about all things—all things that are 'not apparent' to us—we require belief of some kind. The habitual practice of belief is faith. But what we see here are two related meanings of the term 'faith'. It can mean a 'belief that something is true' or it can mean faith in the trustworthiness of another person.

In the first sense, faith is the kind of assent to the truths that we do not know with certainty. I might assent to the claim that my car needs a new oxygen sensor when my mechanic tells me that's why the 'check engine' light is on. On my own, I don't have certainty that this is the case. But I can only have this faith to the degree that I think my mechanic is trustworthy in telling me what's wrong with my car. We see then that faith can also be understood as a kind of habitual trust that the object of our belief continues to be true regardless of various changes in circumstances. I may, for example, have faith—in spite of current evidence to the contrary—that good people are happier than the wicked. My continued trust sustains me through difficult times when my character is unfairly attacked. But faith also conveys a deeper meaning of trusting in a person.

In the Jewish tradition, Abraham offers the best example of this latter kind of faith. God calls Abraham from the land of Ur to a 'place that God will show him'. He listens and trusts God. He packs up his family and they leave for parts unknown. Over the years at various times God makes promises to Abraham—and he habitually believes God. God even promises to 'make a great nation' of him; but Abraham and his wife Sarah have doubts since Sarah cannot conceive. In fact, when God makes this promise to Abraham, Sarah laughs. God hears it and insists they will name their son Isaac ('laughter'). And God fulfils the promise made to them, even though it takes many years of waiting.

Theologian Rowan Williams sees faith in terms of a God in whom we can place our trust. This personal dimension serves as an analogue for how we trust other people. So faith, then, for Abraham is continued reliance on and trust in God. But faith as trust is closely tied to hope, which also sustains us—but in a different manner.

Hope

We often hope for many different sorts of things: a new home, a promotion at the office, a good scotch at the end of the day, or even a reconciliation with a friend from whom we have been alienated. The range of things we hope for covers a very broad spectrum. In light of that, it is helpful first to distinguish hope from a kind of 'wishful thinking'. It is also important to think of it in terms of both an emotion that we might have for any particular good, and as a theological virtue.

First, if we recall that a virtue is a stable disposition to think, feel, and act in particular sorts of ways, we see that mere 'wishing' for something is not the virtue of hope. I may wish to win the lottery but I do not hope for it. Since there is very little chance of winning, I do not invest my emotional or financial efforts in the expectation of my winnings. And this reveals something about the usual definition of hope. Aquinas defines hope generally as the 'patient expectation of a difficult but possible future good'. Although the winnings are a real good, there is almost no mathematical possibility of winning. I am more likely to be struck by lightning on consecutive Thursdays. But if hope is not merely wishful thinking, what is it that distinguishes it from this unrealistic attitude?

Aquinas's general definition applies to both the emotion of hope and the virtue of hope. Our friend Aaron asks us to go on a long hike with him. The trek will be long and hot, but his brother will be there at the end of the trail with cold beer. As the day wears on we become very thirsty. We can imagine the beer quenching our parched palates. We need patience as the beer is not already present. We recognize the pursuit of the beer as difficult since we can only achieve it by finishing the hike. We view the beer as possible, in the sense that we can complete the hike. We understand the beer as 'in the future' since it can only be consumed at the end of the trek. And we understand the beer as a genuine, but material, good. As the Guinness advert claims, 'It's good for you'! We experience the emotion of hope in this case. But this isn't yet the virtue of hope because the object of our hope is merely a good as desired by the appetite—after all, bears and dogs also hope for liquid refreshment.

Hope, considered as a theological virtue, sees God as the referent but also as the facilitator. The 'difficult but possible future good' for the virtue of hope is God and our ultimate union with God, not any specific material good. Union with God and the goods God offers us are what we hope *for*; but we also hope *in* God as one who assists us in our hope. That is, our efforts are not ours alone. Since hope is a theological virtue we are encouraged and strengthened by God in our efforts. If we were to imagine rowing a boat in a river, we can see that we make progress towards our destination by the effort in using the oars. But we are also aided by the current in the river. The effort we make and the movement of the water ideally work in concert together to get us to our destination. The theological virtue of hope is like this—we make an effort—but the effort is aided by divine power when our efforts are in the right direction.

Hope defends us against two different kinds of vice: despair and presumption. We can despair in failing to understand the good as actually attainable or we can presume that we already possess it—which is a kind of arrogance. Those who think that the object of their hope is already in their possession commit a kind of hubris—they presume that they already possess a good they do not. This is taken up in the vice of pride. But there are also those at the other end of the spectrum: those who despair.

Those who fall into despair are those who have patterned their lives in ways that consistently refuse to see the good they desire as 'possible'. They have refused the help that God and others offer. Hope means realizing that the human and divine goods are only possible through the assistance of grace—mediated to us by God and God's representatives.

Nelson Mandela was unjustly imprisoned in a South African jail for twenty-seven years. The young Mandela vigorously opposed the racist system of Apartheid and incurred the wrath of the government. He was arrested for insurrection and incarcerated without trial. In confinement, Mandela could see that his release was a 'difficult, but possible future good'. His patience, however, would require twenty-seven years of separation from his family. Yet, his friends—ministers and others—would visit him regularly offering words of encouragement during his imprisonment. It was through their ministrations, and Mandela seeing them as representing God's faithfulness to him in prison, that he was able to maintain hope during his imprisonment. Without hope rooted in the trustworthiness of God—mediated to him by those who encouraged and strengthened him—Mandela would not have endured. In a letter to his wife, he writes, 'Difficulties break some men but make others. No axe is sharp enough to cut the soul of a sinner who keeps on trying, one armed with the hope that he will rise even in the end.' Hope is an emotion. But it's also a theological virtue that directs him to a good that God has ordained for him and that God helps him to achieve.

Charity

The English word 'love' carries with it many different meanings, ranging from merely liking something—such as gelato—to the very profound self-sacrificial love a parent may have for their child in their willingness to die for that child. The Latin terms for love provide various clues to the different meanings of how we think about this difficult word. The generic term is *amor*—from which the Romans derived the term *amicitia*, 'friendship'. The term *dilectio* has the meaning of 'desire', as in when we desire or are attracted to any particular good. But *caritas* carries the meaning of self-giving sacrificial love that helps distinguish it from both kinship and the desire for sexual union.

The natural love, or affinity, we have for our blood relatives is based partly upon our biological nature wherein we find a greater bond with those to whom we are related. Kin-selection theory suggests that preferences based on closer genetic relationships can be found throughout the animal kingdom, as we see in chimps, dogs, and ants. And for humans, we see that mothers, fathers, siblings, and children all often provide us with an opportunity to love those close in proximity to us. But this is not really a virtue; it is more a natural tendency that we find in all social animals from bees to naked mole rats.

Like other animals, we have a desire for sexual reproduction. The desire itself should not be called 'love' but needs to be further differentiated from 'sexual impulse' since other mammals also have this desire. We should not call the mere desire for sex or reproduction a virtue. It is merely a desire based upon our animal nature. We do find a natural desire for intimacy with others, and human sexuality provides us with that opportunity. But love, considered as a theological virtue, has more in common with friendship.

Among all the human goods, Aristotle valued friendship among the most important. It is central to the well-being of the individual and contributes to the good of the community; it is a kind of participation in the life of 'another self'. He describes its value in the following:

> For without friends no one would choose to live, though he had all other goods…In poverty and in other misfortunes men think friends are the only refuge. It helps the young, too, to keep from error; it aids older people by ministering to their needs and supplementing the activities that are failing from weakness; those in the prime of life it stimulates to noble actions…Friendship seems too to hold states together.

Aristotle distinguishes a number of different kinds of friendship, depending on the goods that the relationship is based on. For him, the highest kind of friendship is both between people of great virtue and based on virtue. They reciprocally will the moral good for each other. But Aristotle never would have dreamed of thinking that a human being—even an extraordinarily virtuous human being—could have 'friendship' with God. Yet this is exactly the imagery the Jewish and Christian thinkers suggest. If friendship is a kind of participation that friends have in one another's lives, this provides an analogy for thinking about how humans can have a love with, for, and in God. That is, love (as charity) is a kind of 'participation' in the life of God. Friends participate in one another's lives as they share common interests, goals, and activities. In the case of charity, humans participate in the goals and activities that God offers.

As a theological virtue, charity is a friendship with God by which we love God for God's own sake and love all those whom God loves. This definition reflects the basic teachings of Judaism in the *Shemá*: 'You shall love the Lord your God with all your heart, mind and strength and your neighbour as yourself.' There is then a twofold object of charity: God and neighbour. And the manner in which we love both is significant.

There are two ways we can consider this love for God and others. In one way, we can love God for the good things God does for us. Since we value our lives, the goods of friends and family, the various pleasures and joys that come our way, we love God for what God does for us. But we can also love God in a second way: for who God is. We can love God for God's own sake regardless of what God does for us. In the Jewish Scriptures, the Satan claims that Job loves God for the riches, prosperity, and success God has bestowed upon Job—and that this is the sole reason Job loves God. But a person can also love God for who God is, and this is why Job continues to love, have faith in, and hope in God even when his external goods are taken away. Job's story demonstrates the kind of unconditional love that distinguishes charity from other forms of love. Kinship bases its love on familiarity, proximity, and relatedness. Sexual desire bases its love on attractiveness. And even human friendship bases its love on shared interests and therefore has a kind of contingent nature to it. But charity remains constant even though none of these other features is present. Kierkegaard puts it this way, 'Erotic love is determined by the object; friendship is determined by the object; only love to one's neighbor is determined by love. Since one's neighbor is every man, unconditionally every man, all distinctions are indeed removed from the object.' We see here the connection between love for God and love for one's neighbour made explicit.

As he describes charity, Aquinas says that we love God and we love others for God's sake. To make this point more clearly, he offers an analogy. Suppose I have a good friend—a friend for whom I would do anything. The friend has children whom I have never met. The friend asks me to care for their children in case anything harmful ever happens to them. For their sake, I love the children whom I have never met. And so charity—which is unconditional, since it's a theological virtue—extends beyond seeing only my family and friends as my neighbours to seeing every other human being as my neighbour.

During the Second World War, in addition to the millions of Jews who were sent to concentration camps, many eastern Europeans were also imprisoned and executed at these same death camps. One such Polish prisoner sent to Auschwitz was Fr Maximilian Kolbe. Prior to his arrest, he had organized resistance to the Nazis. In an attempt to co-opt him, the Nazis offered him citizenship based on the German origins of his name; but he refused and was later sent to prison with others who opposed the Nazis. As many of the prisoners faced death by starvation, Kolbe volunteered to die in the place of one man who had a family.

For Kolbe, the theological virtue of love extended beyond his own self-interest, family, and friends even to strangers. That is, as he saw it, his love for God (and with the guidance of the infused virtue of prudence) led him to think that this act of self-sacrifice was the inevitable conclusion of a life that was consistently devoted to the care and concern for others.

Chapter 6
The capital vices: love gone wrong

Vices as bad habits

A vice is a relatively stable disposition to behave badly; or in Aristotle's words, 'a vice is a bad habit of the soul'. It is a constitutional defect in our nature that prevents us from pursuing and achieving genuine goods constitutive of human flourishing in appropriate ways. The capital vices, as they are traditionally known, occupy an important role as a source for the other vices because their influence seems to afflict us to a greater degree than other vices. They often feed off one another and give birth to other vices. In their most typical listing, the capital vices are pride, envy, avarice, wrath, sloth, gluttony, and lust. In this chapter we consider the capital vices and look at ways in which some of the virtues can correct the harm that these vices do.

A common experience many people have concerns the uncomfortable encounters they have on social media platforms with self-appointed 'experts' who police, correct, and ridicule all those with whom they disagree. An example is Jack, a 75-year-old pensioner who spends much of his time online. He taps into racist webpages, collects memes that perfectly suit his own unacknowledged biases, and angrily insists that all news outlets that do not agree with his own pre-conceived ideas are 'fake news'. Jack pounces on his unsuspecting interlocutors with unbridled wrath as he unleashes a torrent of personal attacks and irrelevancies. He secretly envies those who know more than he does, and it gnaws away at him. Yet, his perpetual sloth prevents him from ever taking the effort to learn anything more than what he already thinks he knows. And behind all of this stands his pride: a pride that never admits mistakes, a pride that ridicules his enemies, and a pride that looks down upon all the poorly informed and misled masses. He alone knows the truth. Jack exhibits many of the vices. Even worse, many of his vices feed upon one another in unhealthy ways that provoke him to further bad behaviour. Unfortunately, Jack is not alone in his vice.

Since human beings are creatures of habit, and since we develop these habits over time, we can develop bad ones as well as good ones. Jack, for example, did not develop his pride, wrath, and sloth in an instant but he let them take hold of his life without intervention. Parents and friends may have tried to admonish him, but to no avail. Most philosophers and moral psychologists would agree that it is much easier to develop bad habits than it is to develop good ones. If you were to walk into a bookshop and go to the 'Self-Improvement' section, you would make an interesting discovery. There are no books on how to increase your opioid addiction, no volumes on how to be a more irritating partner, no guides on how to be a completely ineffective parent, no manuals on how to provoke people online, and no anthologies on how to increase your arrogance. Instead, what self-improvement presupposes is that we have a natural tendency to give in to our desires and to leave them unchecked. We have a disturbing ability to make the wrong choices, leading to the formation of bad habits. Conversely, virtue is hard work. It taxes us and takes considerable effort to form. And it means actively fighting against the inertia of our deeply ingrained bad habits and destructive desires.

When we distinguish between virtues and vices we can think of them in terms of appropriate or inappropriate ways of pursuing various goods, or whether or not our activities are excessively self-centred to the point of denying the legitimate claims of others. An important point to remember is that these capital vices arise out of our finite condition as creatures that have specific needs and desires, and that those desires orient us to our various goods. The vices are, therefore, a result of 'love gone wrong'.

In the traditional list of the vices, pride was the most serious—Augustine and Aquinas saw it as standing behind all the other capital vices. But envy of another's good and excessive desire for wealth caused by avarice both corrupt the soul and alienate the self from others. Wrath, sloth, gluttony, and lust all concern the individual's mastery over herself and her desires. The vices, as we consider them, proceed from the most damaging, pride, to those primarily concerned with our animality, namely gluttony and lust. Yet, each one is destructive of the self and of the self's relationships with others.

Pride

When we speak of pride, we immediately confront a problem of definition. Is it wrong for me to be proud of my child when she does well in school? It would be odd to say that this is vicious since it seems to be a natural response that harms no one and rightly recognizes an important good of accomplishment. We can, therefore, distinguish between proper pride and wicked pride. Proper pride may include the kind of satisfaction of a job well done, the sense of self-confidence needed to achieve morally good aspirations, or the kind of dignity and regard all people should have for themselves. Proper pride is not a vice, as it is not antithetical to our flourishing. But wicked pride is what we see in people who are haughty, arrogant, vain, or condescending. These are the people who grasp for more importance than they deserve or who illicitly elevate themselves above others.

To understand how pride becomes vicious we need to recall Aristotle's basic idea that all people desire their own good and they act accordingly. The desire for any good is not in itself evil but part of our nature as creatures with needs. In order to sustain our own existence, we must pursue those things that are genuinely good for us. We all desire our own excellence, but when our desires exceed what is appropriate they become vicious. And we can think of this viciousness either in terms of a theological dimension or in terms of a more ordinary moral dimension. Aquinas captures these two dimensions when he says that pride can be understood either as 'rebellion against God' or as an 'illicit desire for pre-eminence'. In the theological sense of pride, it is a kind of immoral contention with God. The person not only does not recognize God as God but wants to usurp God. In the moral sense of pride, the individual wants ascendancy over others in ways that harm individuals within their community.

Judaism and Christianity both see the theological dimension of pride in their depictions of Satan, who refuses to worship God and becomes jealous of humanity, and Iblis is a similar figure in Islamic theology. The traditional narrative takes poetic shape in Milton's *Paradise Lost*, where Satan is portrayed as a creature who overreaches what is appropriate for him; he is not satisfied to be a creature but wants to be God. He proclaims that it would be 'better to reign in hell than serve in heaven'. Pride directly opposes the order God has established; and Satan wants dominance, not community. When this happens, one has replaced the love of God with an inordinate love of self. In this theological understanding, since we were created for the purpose of loving God as our supreme end, we are unable to achieve that end. The Qur'ān says that 'Arrogance means rejecting the truth and looking down on people.' And when we set ourselves over and against others we have no choice but to 'look down' on them. This condescension need not be a religious attempt to usurp God but could be any kind of illicit elevation of the self over others.

Regardless of any religious commitments, people seem to universally find the 'moral version' of pride objectionable, especially when they see others grasping for illicit pre-eminence. This ranges from the everyday occurrences of colleagues claiming more credit than they merit to Donald Trump, who regularly claims that he is better at everything than everybody. Note that Trump's boasts are not at all like, for example, the boxer Muhammad Ali, who declared himself 'The Greatest' when he actually was with regard to his expertise as a pugilist. People like Trump, however, claim for themselves pre-eminence they do not truly possess—and this derives from a false value they ascribe to themselves.

We can differentiate three specific kinds of pride: vanity, conceit, and arrogance. All involve a disproportionate desire for pre-eminence, but in different ways. Vanity requires an audience. The vain person perpetually needs to be the centre of attention. Conceit requires a comparison to others in a way that elevates the individual over all other competitors. And the arrogant simply consider themselves superior to others without bothering to investigate the competition. The narcissistic tendencies of all three of these versions of pride support the social science research that points to narcissists being excessively competitive, aggressive, domineering, angry, and hostile to others. As a result, the desire for pre-eminence naturally results in feelings of isolation and alienation from their communities. Humility has historically been viewed as the cure for pride. The same research indicates that since humble people lack the excessive desire for pre-eminence, they tend to value others much more than the proud do and so they also have healthier relationships (Figure 9).

Humility is that inward disposition that enables people to rightly value themselves as they ought. It provides a corrective to pride since it guards against the unhealthy overreaching we are tempted towards. Since pride desires a kind of inordinate excellence for the soul at the expense of others, humility tempers this desire by helping us to embrace our rightful place in the overall scheme of our various relationships. It provides a check on our tendency to

gracia · uires hosticas cueruantium · quid iudith in holoferne · quem di
cere possimus totum infernum · quasi qui mehl supernu habeat
quid iabel in sysara madianitarum principe fecerunt · que ualentia
seruis infirmious mehl aliud est · nisi quod humilitas semper pre
ualet superbie in quacumqz sconim professione ·

9. The way to conquer the vice of pride is to destroy it through the
acquisition of the virtue of humility.

falsely inflate our own value and importance. Maimonides even goes so far as to equate humility with piety and wisdom itself. Where pride creates a kind of moral distance between ourselves and others, humility heals us—and our relationships with others—by providing a bridge where we see others as possessing the same kind of value we ascribe to ourselves.

Envy

As with pride, envy also has a virtuous meaning. Theologian Krister Stendahl coined the term 'holy envy' wherein people could desire the good qualities of others and take the necessary steps to acquire them for themselves. If we think about the admirable qualities of Bishop Desmond Tutu with regard to his zeal for justice, his considerable patience, his care for the outcasts, and his sense of forgiveness, he can be seen as a moral exemplar. 'Holy envy' is an admirable trait since it is a kind of self-improvement motivated by a good in another that intends no harm to the other. But in contrast to holy envy we should consider vicious envy, which is often conflated with jealousy.

The jealous person is one who has a relationship with another and fears losing it. People are jealous of others in ways that differ from desiring a quality or a possession. I am not jealous of another person's dog, or home, or car; I am jealous of another person's attention that is directed to someone other than me. A person, for example, usually does not want their partner's attention inordinately directed to another potential lover.

Envy, as distinguished from jealousy, is a kind of sadness 'over another's good'. We all believe we deserve to possess specific goods in life, including self-esteem, status, and personal abilities. This desire is not, in itself, evil. However, when we become obsessed with the good fortune of others, it turns to envy. The envious are those who become disturbed over another's good fortune, possessions, talents, abilities, or success. Envy involves the repeated comparison of the self to others in a way that is always destructive. Envy cuts people off from one another, since the comparison of the self to others results in a person wanting evil things to happen to other people. A kind of self-satisfied *Schadenfreude* can eventually replace the original desire for the object or the status. Envy involves harbouring resentment towards another so that one can feel better about oneself. A community can be destroyed by envy, since the one who practises envy can only be satisfied when others have lost their pre-eminence.

An important way that envy manifests itself is with regard to another's status or possessions. In a way that demonstrates the inverse of holy envy, 'status envy' is a kind of resentment over another person's qualities or position. Shakespeare's *Othello* provides an illuminating look at status envy. Iago—a soldier who strives for advancement and prestige—is passed over for a promotion to lieutenant for one who is (in his mind) a lesser person, Cassio. Iago envies Cassio's status as lieutenant, which he thinks should have rightfully been his own appointment. Cassio does not possess a particular item or object. Iago envies Cassio's status as favoured by Othello. But status envy is but one of two kinds—we can also envy others for what they possess.

The evil creature Gollum in Tolkien's *The Lord of the Rings* suffers from 'object envy'—sometimes called 'covetousness'. Gollum comes into possession of this great Ring that turns the bearer invisible—but it also grants power to those who can wield it. His desire for the Ring consumes him to the point of his own destruction. He loses the Ring and discovers the hobbit Bilbo Baggins now possesses it. He envies Bilbo's status because the hobbit is the new owner of the Ring—but mostly he envies Bilbo because of what Bilbo possesses. And his envy of Bilbo quickly turns to hatred. He shouts after Bilbo, as the hobbit makes his escape, 'We hates it. We hates it forever.' Envy turns to hatred and for this reason is listed among the capital vices. To prevent envy and its offspring hatred, we need to learn to care for others as we do for ourselves.

10. The envious, like Circe, direct their attention—and hatred—towards others since others possess something the envious do not.

Kindness is that habit that facilitates our care for others. It is a movement from competition to contentedness, or even a solidarity with others. Instead of seeing another person's qualities or property as a threat to me, I see the other person as 'another self'. Genuine friendship enables a person to see the other's good—as much as one can—as one's own good. Instead of resenting and hating the other, a person fully participates in the joy of the other. But this can only be done when I no longer see the other as a threat to my own good (Figure 10). This requires a movement of the moral imagination away from obsessive desire to a consideration of a person who deserves respect and even love.

Avarice

When Aristotle considered different conceptions for the human good, he listed health, pleasure, and wealth as the main competitors to flourishing. He noted that wealth is a good but it is merely an instrumental good. It is good for the things we can do with it, but we do not desire it for its own sake. There is nothing in the material qualities of metal or paper that is desirable in itself. Wealth is 'good' to the extent to which it can help us secure other goods that we need. It enables us to purchase food and shelter for ourselves and others: family, friends, and those without sufficient financial means of their own. But a desire for wealth—when not properly ordered to other goods, or when directed excessively to the self—becomes destructive; it is this excessive focus on wealth and the manner in which we use it that lies at the heart of avarice.

Avarice, or 'greed', is the disposition to excessively desire money or possessions. Possessions do indeed enable us to live as embodied creatures, since these things provide us with the necessities of life. However, it is entirely possible that the desire for these goods can become all-consuming desire. Avarice is the internal disposition to pursue the instrumental good of wealth to the exclusion of healthy human relationships. The individual sees the instrumental good as an intrinsic good; as a result human relationships are often sacrificed for economic success. We become preoccupied with the acquisition of wealth rather than with concern for others since avarice undermines our ability to genuinely care for others. The pursuit of wealth at the expense of all other goods leaves no room for any other values.

With avarice we see a compulsive desire for more and more: a desire that is never satisfied. When asked how much wealth was enough Rockefeller responded with 'Just a little bit more'. The person in the throes of avarice thinks that wealth will provide an inner sense of well-being, but it does not. It only feeds the desire even more—as we might expect with a bad habit of the soul.

In Charles Dickens's book *A Christmas Carol*, Ebenezer Scrooge provides a helpful example of the person consumed with avarice. As Scrooge looks back on his life with the help of the various ghosts, he sees that at every critical juncture, when confronted with a choice between wealth and persons, he chose wealth. His decision to work on holidays, when others enjoyed companionship with their loved ones, turned him into a resentful person. Over the years, he loses every personal relationship he has ever had. He has business 'relationships' but no spouse or friends. He becomes immune to the call of compassion. When his nephew wishes him a 'Merry Christmas', he responds with, 'If I could work my will...every idiot who goes about with "Merry Christmas" on his lips, should be boiled with his own pudding, and buried with a stake of holly through his heart.' And when others ask for charity, Scrooge tells them that the poor should simply die and reduce the 'surplus population'. Avarice precludes compassion.

A person can hoard their wealth like Scrooge, or spend it in profligate ways. The pop star who seeks fame for the purpose of great wealth is also greedy. He might use the wealth not for the purpose of hoarding but for lavish spending on himself in terms of exotic cars, multiple mansions, and the finest food and drink. The profligate is liberal with the wealth in a wasteful rather than in a good way.

Liberality can also be thought of as a virtue—as letting go and unclenching the fist—but not in a careless or unthoughtful manner. The key is in understanding the inner disposition and its relationship to the others. When confronted with the tragic illness of Tiny Tim, Scrooge imagines a world where Tim does not die but lives. He is drawn in through compassion and transforms from a person who is overly attached to his wealth to a person whose affections orient to his neighbours; he begins to 'love his neighbour as himself'. After his 'conversion', he gladly gives to the Cratchit family—he knows they need money and he provides it. His liberality is other-focused but also attentive to their specific needs. The love and care for persons has replaced the love of money.

Wrath

In a similar way that the mere desire for wealth is not avarice, so too the emotion of anger should not be identified with the vice of wrath (*ira*). We should make a distinction among three kinds of anger: emotional anger, virtuous anger, and vicious anger. First, emotional anger is a visceral response to a perceived threat to either ourselves or to others. I can be angered by the bugs that seem to see me as food for their evening meal. This is neither virtuous nor vicious—it is merely my emotional response to insects. Second, I may be virtuously angered when I read of workers in factories who have died due to unsafe, illegal, and inhumane working conditions. This is an anger prompted by the demands of justice. Al-Ghazzali says that anger is often a helpful tool. But when our anger is excessive and resembles a fire that burns our heart and clouds our reason, the tool is used against ourselves and becomes a vice. This third kind of anger, vicious anger, is wrath. And wrath can come about in a variety of ways.

A person can respond in anger too quickly, as in the case of seeming to hear resentment in the voice of one's partner. Or a person can respond with excessive anger, as in the case of a parent who overreacts to her child breaking a dish. Or a person can respond in anger to the wrong object, as in the case of a worker who comes home after a frustrating day and yells at the dog. But a person can also respond in anger by harbouring resentment for years, as in the case of a child who never forgives her parents for moving her away from her friends when she was young. When any of these kinds of anger becomes a relatively fixed feature of one's character it has become a vice.

In every instance of wrath there is one constant: the idea that an injustice has been committed and must not go unheeded. What is distinctive about wrath is that it exceeds what is appropriate, given the circumstances. There are two ways in which this happens: angry outbursts and seething resentment.

The angry outbursts are the more recognizable form of wrath as a person reacts to a situation out of proportion to the cause. A person in the grip of wrath has her moral perceptions radically altered so that she cannot grasp situations as they really are. The anger rises so that the person can become both physically and emotionally 'heated'. People consumed with anger are often described as 'burning with wrath'. Like Al-Ghazzali, Dante took the idea of 'heat' and connected it to how smoke inhibits the vision of wrathful souls in the *Purgatorio*.

Angry outbursts are the more obvious forms of wrath, but hidden resentment can also function as a kind of wrath. This form accumulates gradually over time. Instead of giving free rein to my anger in violent and obvious verbal or physical demonstrations, I might prefer to keep this vice hidden from others by nursing it privately. The Confucian tradition sees this kind of wrath as a poison that harms the self by its constant attention to the alleged harm.

The cure for wrath is in practising a kind of patient and gentle self-control. The patient person, the person who can master their anger, possesses two important qualities that the wrathful person does not. First, an ability to know what kinds of provocations deserve an appropriately and virtuously angry response. Second, the habituated ability to control her own anger in ways that neither harm herself nor others.

The patiently gentle person is not easily angered, but knows those harms that truly deserve an angry response, such as genocide, sexual abuse, or political corruption. The patient person responds appropriately, or proportionately, to genuine provocations with neither too much nor too little reaction. And as philosopher Rebecca Konyndyk DeYoung notes, the cultivation of a humble kind of gentleness is what restrains the urge to give free rein to one's wrath. Resisting the temptation to harbour long-standing resentments, gentle people habitually forgive others.

Sloth

The traditional view of sloth (*acedia*) is that of lazy people who cannot seem to rouse themselves to any significant effort, and so condemn themselves to their own destruction. Aesop's fable of the ant and the grasshopper portrays this understanding well. The ant works diligently throughout the summer, harvesting and saving up plenty of food for the long winter ahead, while the grasshopper idles away the hours taunting the ant. But when winter comes the lazy grasshopper dies of starvation while the ant survives. This is how most people think of sloth as it seems to call us to an excessive 'rest'. If this captured the nature of sloth, then the 'cure' would seem to be a kind of industriousness. This, however, is a truncated understanding of sloth.

Certain forms of 'busyness' are also sloth in the sense that *acedia* is a kind of *resistance to the demands of love*. This resistance can be seen in 'busying' the self with trivialities and amusements in the case of the teen who spends all of his time focused on social media and video games. But it can also be seen in the professional who devotes all of their time at the office working on important projects while neglecting their family. Sloth makes people callous to the demands of love since it distracts people from the difficult work of fulfilling their responsibilities. Love demands not neglecting others (and one's own self) by being overly occupied with distractions.

Sloth differs from the other capital vices in the sense that it consists in the avoidance of the good rather than the inappropriate pursuit of some good. As such, it tends toward distraction. A person in the grip of sloth avoids what they should be doing at all costs. Life becomes a constant distraction. In this regard, sloth represents a kind of inner inertia where an individual cannot rouse themselves to do what they should. They prefer 'something other' than the good they should be doing.

Evagrius, the 4th-century monk, describes this well when he discusses the monk who will attend to anything but what he should. He describes *acedia* in terms of being a demon that torments the soul of the monk.

> First of all, he makes it appear that the sun moves slowly or not at all, and that the day appears to be 50 hours long... And further, he instills in him a dislike... for his state of life itself, for manual labor, and also the idea that love has disappeared from among the brothers and there is no one to console him... He leads him on to a desire for other places where he can easily find the wherewithal to meet his needs and pursue a trade that is easier and more productive.

The monk who suffers from *acedia* will do anything but what he is supposed to do. He seeks out distractions to the neglect of his calling. From this, the monk becomes 'downcast'. The slothful person experiences a sadness of the soul because they cannot find satisfaction in any of their distractions. If nothing will bring them happiness, they eventually experience despair, which is harmful to a person's good as they no longer see the possibility of any good thing bringing happiness.

Diligence, not busyness, is the cure for sloth. Diligence is a kind of commitment to do the good. It is a form of 'love for the good' that helps us overcome sloth. It is not merely the wishing to do the good, but the repeated practice of forcing oneself to do the good and the attendant desire for doing the good. I must be able to recognize in myself instances of avoidance. A kind of moral and mental vigilance must be practised in order not to give in to the many distractions that tempt me from doing what I ought. The diligent soul is the one that overcomes—not by more work, but by more care for that which she should.

Gluttony and lust

The desires for food and sex are similar in that both derive from our animal nature. And over time, societies have occasionally either glorified or demonized these desires. We cannot live without the basic goods of food and drink; and Maslow's 'hierarchy of needs' places them at the very foundation so that they become central to our lives and many of our activities. The desires themselves orient us to genuine goods; but these goods are 'lower' than both an individual's overall well-being and the 'common goods' of peace and justice that a society needs to flourish. When considering the various higher and lower goods that people pursue, John Stuart Mill quipped that 'It is better to be a human being dissatisfied than a pig satisfied; better to be Socrates dissatisfied than a fool satisfied. And if the fool, or the pig, is of a different opinion, it is only because they only know their own side of the question.' What Mill saw was that some 'animal goods'—although they are truly good—do not suffice for a well-lived life. Both the desires for food and for sex—by themselves—do not offer fulfilment. The vices of gluttony and lust correspond to these two excessive desires.

Popular media often represent gluttony in terms of excessive eating, obesity, or copious consumption. Like all the vices, gluttony concerns a basic good that is either pursued inordinately, or for the wrong reasons. Aristotle argues that the amount of food we consume is always 'relative to us'. But gluttony takes us beyond that which is commended by right reason to the excessive desire for the pleasures that only food and drink can provide. The focus here for the person is on the desire itself, which makes it more difficult for us to participate in relationships that require an 'other regarding' focus. For Aquinas, 'Gluttony primarily and intrinsically signifies the intemperate desire to consume food, not the consumption of food itself.' This may seem like a small distinction but it is significant. Food and drink are genuine goods. Rather, the problem is the importance and centrality they occupy in our lives.

This excessive fixation on how we regard food and drink and their appropriate place in our lives can be understood in the contrast between the person who 'lives to eat' and the one who 'eats to live'. Gluttons take a good intended as a means to good living and make it the end in itself. If our sole purpose is to gratify our own pleasures of the palate other people take on a secondary status.

Gluttony might not consist merely in the quantity of food consumed or in the manner that we consume it; it might also encompass the manner in which it is produced and the ways the production affects others. A society fixated on the convenient and the inexpensive without concerns for the environment or the poor might be 'gluttonous' as long as the only consideration is the priority of the individual's satisfaction. An internal attachment to the convenient and inexpensive may be so strong that issues of compassion and justice are excluded from discussion. After all, we would rather have our burgers than worry about the deforestation of the habitat of indigenous peoples or the manner in which cattle are treated.

The fact is that we cannot live without food. And while some of us might *feel* as if we cannot live without sex, this is not so. Of all the traditional vices, lust may be the most controversial. After all, if sex is a human good why call its pursuit a vice? The recent reversal of lust from a vice to a virtue for some thinkers is their way of claiming a kind of independence from a puritanical heritage they have unwillingly inherited. Yet, upon a little reflection, this is misguided in at least two ways. First, it misrepresents the tradition since this tradition considers sexual reproduction to be a good created by God. Second, it fails to see the potential harms irresponsible sexual behaviour or desire can cause.

Sex, as a basic human good, is pleasurable, pro-creative, and can lead to interpersonal bonding. For those with a religious perspective, it is a celebration of God's goodness to humanity. But regardless of religious convictions, most people will agree that unrestrained and indiscriminate sexual activity can be harmful to the self as well as to others. Moreover, since we are humans, we tend to see sexual activity as not merely the function of instinct but requiring the direction of right reason.

Human sexuality—considered from the perspective of morally responsible behaviour—requires a consideration of the appropriate person, context, and purpose. The consent of an adult person is the absolute minimum of appropriate sexual relations and in many cultural and religious traditions the requirement is that the consenting adult is one's spouse. An appropriate context requires discretion. And an appropriate intent may be the procreation of life, mutual intimacy, or some other non-coercive, person-affirming attitude. But all of this should be seen within a wider vision of a good life. That is, sexual activity is not, at least in the virtue tradition, the greatest of all goods. For Aristotle, pleasure should not be the sole purpose of a human life since human beings have goods that transcend mere animality. A person who is utterly unable to control their sexual appetites is a threat to a community and to its most vulnerable members.

A person consumed with lust wants the experience of sex and does not genuinely consider the partner as a person. The person is objectified. Love, as a relationship to the other, is replaced with sex as an act with an object. One's sexual 'partner' is no longer viewed as a reciprocal giver and receiver of pleasure but as a mere aid to autoeroticism. The Jewish philosopher Martin Buber would call this an 'I–It' relationship and a failure to practise the 'I–Thou' relationship. Paradoxically, sex without love as an act of intimacy drives people further apart. That is, the more sex without love, the more isolated people become since a person achieves only the semblance of intimacy rather than the real thing. Philosopher Josef Pieper remarked that for the person consumed with lust, 'The aim should be a maximum of pleasure with a minimum of personal involvement.' With lust, the other person is used as a means and then promptly discarded when convenient. Lust cannot deliver on the satisfaction it promises. Søren Kierkegaard, the 19th-century Danish philosopher, created a character he called 'The Seducer' who, after many sexual encounters, came to realize that hedonic satisfaction diminished with each and every sexual conquest. But in order to combat lust, an individual needs to see the other as a person and not merely as a source of gratification.

Lust and gluttony both distort our perception and pursuit of sex and food. These desires—in order not to become dominant forces in our lives—require the moderating influence of temperance—which helps us to see their proper place in a well-lived life: as real human goods but not as 'goodness itself'. The vices shed light on the virtues by showing us those avenues of behaviour that lead to a disintegration of the self and of our communities. They demonstrate how any one particular good can distort our perception, our deliberation, and our character.

Conclusion

It is helpful to recall that virtues and vices admit of varying degrees in different populations, and so we should expect some variability in how and when people possess them. Contrast the 6-year-old beginning cellist, for example, with the master Yo-Yo Ma. The beginner stumbles through the shortest of works, missing notes, rushing at times, and slowing down and speeding up according to her abilities. Ma, however, is a *virtuoso*. He is a 'musical exemplar'. He plays all the right notes, at the right time, in the right tempo, at the right volume, in the right way. He is an exceptionally rare talent who has devoted countless hours to his craft. But between the novice and virtuoso are countless others: the 12-year-old who is admitted to the local youth symphony, the university student who plays in her school's production of Handel's *Messiah*, and the schoolteacher who supplements her income with lessons to the beginners. This range of abilities is what we should also expect with the virtues.

The survey of the virtues covered so far presents what many people think is the collected wisdom of centuries of reflection—not on music, but on good habits of character. The virtues may vary with cultural and religious contexts but still demonstrate considerable continuity in terms of their descriptions. People we know tend to behave in fairly predictable ways and this behaviour has at its core a stability that reflects their moral character.

Instead of retreating into the background, attention to the virtues has not only gained momentum in traditional theological and philosophical circles but it has found new advocates in the social sciences as well. But with this renaissance of the virtues across the disciplines, there are those who call into question the value of the virtues.

Critics of the virtues suggest a number of problematic features ranging from disagreements about how to understand particular virtues to the competing lists of virtues found in different philosophical or theological systems. Others think that humans simply lack the kinds of robust character traits that might qualify as virtues.

The lists of virtues have varied somewhat from culture to culture, as have their exact definitions. Most cultures see wisdom, justice, compassion, self-control, and friendship as qualities people ought to possess. But if we consider a specific virtue like wisdom, some cultures (and thinkers) see it in a purely secular manner in terms of living a well-regulated life where we control our various appetites, as Cicero and Aristotle suggest, while the Jewish tradition would construe it primarily with regard to our reverence for God and following divine precepts. Not only that, but the relative ranking of the virtues has also varied. Plato saw justice as the most important of the moral virtues, while Aristotle thought it was prudence. And Aquinas argued that charity surpassed both of these. But in the end, there are a cluster of virtues that we all seem to affirm as having some necessary part to play in the good life. Yet two notable exceptions challenged the traditional construal of the virtues and their role: David Hume and Friedrich Nietzsche.

David Hume's approach to morality in general was based upon 'moral sentiment' where moral feelings were central to our deliberation about ethics and so our practical reason was simply a means to best secure the satisfaction of our various desires. On Hume's account only those habits that led to some obvious satisfaction of a desire could be counted as a virtue. Hume denounced some of the traditional virtues as 'monkish' since they seemed to inhibit our pursuit of the good life. For him, religion—and the virtues it encouraged—had bound human beings to pointless exercises in self-denial with the result that they blindly followed the rules and practices dictated to them by their religious leaders. Qualities such as celibacy, fasting, humility, self-denial, and silence were not virtues at all but vices because they do not encourage a person's 'manner of purpose; neither do they advance a man's fortune in the world, nor render him a more valuable member of society; neither qualify him for the entertainment of company, nor increase his power of self-enjoyment'. Yet, even on Hume's own terms, it may be that the cultivation of such virtues as self-control and humility have a place in the good life. Sexual promiscuity could lead to unfortunate consequences where sexual fidelity would not only prevent retribution from jealous partners but could also increase the pleasure itself. Humility might lead to greater life satisfaction. But endorsing Hume's underlying understanding of virtue as satisfying the sentiments of approval or disapproval requires a radical rejection of the traditional understanding that the virtues involve objective excellence.

Like Hume, Nietzsche also rejected traditional accounts of the virtues. Yet he went further by offering a thorough repudiation of them. Nietzsche argues that the traditional virtues are merely terms used and cultivated by the weak to control the strong. He draws up a 'genealogy of morals' and concludes that terms like 'good' and 'evil' have no real meaning apart from self-descriptions of the people who employ them—and the ones who use these terms are weak. They are not only weak, but he adds that, 'Every virtue inclines toward stupidity.'

In place of the traditional virtues, Nietzsche offers his own transformation of Aristotle's 'great-souled man' by suggesting his new moral ideal as 'beyond good and evil'. The *Übermensch* is the one who flatly rejects traditional virtues as fictions and creates his own values based upon his own strength and creativity. Humility and love, for example, were part of the 'slave' morality that Nietzsche detested—introduced by Judaism and brought to its completion in Christianity. He replaces humility with limitless self-expression and love with egoism. All traditional virtues are inverted to favour those qualities that exalt the powerful and creative. Anything that inhibits these impulses should be jettisoned.

Nietzsche, of course, knows that the general population will reject his project since they all praise the traditional virtues, even if they cannot achieve them. But his genealogical analysis seems more wishful thinking on his part than an actual argument. How is it that he alone has been spared from the deception? But more importantly, this rejection of the virtues seems to violate our basic intuitions about good people and their admirable qualities.

Some contemporary psychologists and philosophers have called into question whether or not we can achieve virtues—and if we can't, why should we bother to continue to use virtue language? In the 21st century, both philosophers and psychologists have energetically explored the virtues in terms of empirical research (especially in positive psychology) and in the tradition of analytic ethics. And in parts of both psychology and philosophy, the virtues have been subject to serious criticisms.

Some psychologists, like Daniel Batson, think that virtues are simply beyond the scope of empirical research and do not think that they are helpful for scientific research. Empiricists encounter serious difficulties when they try to describe those internal dispositions constitutive of the virtues. But even in cases where psychologists can study motivation, there seems to be a good deal of self-deception about one's own good motives, thereby undercutting a key element of what a virtue is: we need to be people who not only do the right things in the right ways, but also with the right motives without lying to ourselves.

In a similar way, philosophers Gilbert Harmon and John Doris complain that the virtues seem absent from the general population and, if so, they can't possibly have much value. That is, they think that we should be able to find empirical evidence that people behave in the ways that express the virtues. But psychological experiments fail to show this being present. Specific situations seem to radically alter an individual's decision-making so that consistent traits do not seem to endure across contexts as Aristotle and others claim.

But what Harmon and Doris fail to see is that exemplary moral virtue may be just as rare in the world as Yo-Yo Ma's musical virtuosity. People may possess virtues like humility and self-control in varying degrees and we should not expect the self-control of a 6-year-old or a 25-year-old to be the same as that of a 60-year-old. Neither complete virtue nor total vice but probably something in between is the reasonable expectation in our daily encounters. And this is exactly what we find argued for in the recent work of Christian Miller, who thinks that most people have mixed moral character and that our moral behaviour is largely sensitive to environmental factors that we might not even be aware of.

Given these situational factors, we may have competing impulses in different contexts. When confronted by a person asking for money we might be divided between an impulse towards compassion and another towards justice by observing that the individual making the request has nice clothing. Trying to isolate just one virtue in one context may not be a valid way of proving that virtues do not exist. And given the central role that the virtues have played in a wide range of societies and cultures, we may not want to jettison them just yet.

References

Chapter 1: Whose virtues, which vices?

Aquinas, *Summa Theologiae*, trans. The Fathers of the English
Dominican Province (Benziger Brothers, 1920), IIaIIae 55.

Augustine, *City of God*, trans. Marcus Dods (Hendrickson,
2009), XIX.25.

Iris Murdoch, *The Sovereignty of Good* (Routledge, 1971), 101.

Chapter 2: The moral virtues: feeling good about being good

Aquinas, *Summa Theologiae*, trans. The Fathers of the English
Dominican Province (Benziger Brothers, 1920), IIaIIae 123.11,
IIaIIae 141.2, IIaIIae 149.1, and IIaIIae149.3.

Aristotle, *Nicomachean Ethics*, trans. Terrance Irwin (Hackett, 1999),
1140a27, 1119a16, 1115b17–20, and 1128b22.

Plato, *Republic*, trans. G. M. A. Grube (Hackett, 1992), 473d.

Chapter 3: The intellectual virtues: being mindful

Aristotle, *Metaphysics*, trans. C. D. C. Reeve (Hackett, 2016), 982b.

Justin Kruger and David Dunning, 'Unskilled and Unaware of It: How
Difficulties in Recognizing One's Own Incompetence Lead to
Inflated Self-Assessments', *Journal of Personality and Social
Psychology* (1999), 77.6, p. 1126.

Plato, *Apology*, trans. G. M. A. Grube (Hackett, 2002), 18a and 36c.

Harry Frankfurt, *On Bullshit* (Princeton University Press, 2005), 125.

Plato, *Theaetetus*, trans. John McDowell (Oxford University Press,
2014), 155d.

David Foster Wallace, *This is Water* (Little, Brown and Company, 2009).

Chapter 4: Islamic and Confucian accounts of the virtues

Al-Ghazzali, *Alchemy of Happiness*, trans. Jay R. Crook (Great Books of the Islamic World, 2005), vol. 2 pp. 867f., 453, and 488.

Confucius, *Analects*, trans. D. D. Lau (Penguin, 1979), 4.11 and 3.24.

Mencius, *Mengzi* 2A6, as quoted in P. J. Ivanhoe, *Ehtics in the Confucian Tradition* 2nd edn (Hackett, 2002), 38.

Zisi, *The Doctrine of the Mean*, trans. James Legge (Trübner, 1861), II.1.

Chapter 5: The theological virtues: be good, by God!

Aquinas, *Summa Theologiae*, trans. The Fathers of the English Dominican Province (Benziger Brothers, 1920), IIaIIae 55, IIaIIae 4.1.

Moses Maimonides, *The Guide for the Perplexed*, trans. M. Friedlander (Digireads, 2018), part III, chapter XXVIII.

The quotation from Nelson Mandela comes from a letter he wrote to Winnie Mandela dated 1 February 1975.

Aristotle, *Nicomachean Ethics*, trans. Terrance Irwin (Hackett, 1999), 1155a5–24.

Søren Kierkegaard, *Works of Love* (Harper Perennial 1964), 77.

Charles Dickens, *A Christmas Carol* (Dover, 1991), I.21.

Chapter 6: The capital vices: love gone wrong

Aquinas, *Summa Theologiae*, trans. The Fathers of the English Dominican Province (Benziger Brothers, 1920), IIaIIae 55, IIaIIae 148.1.

Evagrius of Pontus, *The Greek Ascetic Corpus*, trans. Robert Sinkewicz (Oxford University Press, 2006), 99.

Joseph Pieper, *Faith, Hope, Love* (Ignatius Press, 1997), 262f.

John Stuart Mill, *Utilitarianism* (Hackett, 2002), 10.

Conclusion

David Hume, *An Enquiry Concerning Human Understanding* (Oxford World's Classics, 2008), 177.

Friedrich Nietzsche, *The Will to Power*, trans. Anthony Ludovici (Barnes and Noble, 2006), 120.

Friedrich Nietzsche, *Genealogy of Morals*, trans. Douglas Smith (Oxford World's Classics, 2009), 17.

Further reading

Chapter 1: Whose virtues, which vices?

Robert Merrihew Adams, *A Theory of Virtue: Excellence in Being for the Good* (Oxford University Press, 2006).

Aquinas, *Summa Theologiae*, trans. The Fathers of the English Dominican Province (Benziger Brothers, 1920).

Heather Battaly, *Virtue* (Polity, 2015).

Alasdair MacIntyre, *After Virtue* (University of Notre Dame Press, 1981).

Iris Murdoch, *The Sovereignty of Good* (Routledge, 1971).

Kevin Timpe and Craig A. Boyd, *Virtues and their Vices* (Oxford University Press, 2014).

Liezl van Zyl, *Virtue Ethics* (Routledge, 2018).

Chapter 2: The moral virtues: feeling good about being good

Aristotle, *Nicomachean Ethics*, trans. David Ross (Oxford World's Classics, 2009).

Cicero, *On Obligations*, trans. D. B. Walsh (Oxford University Press, 2008).

André Comte-Sponville, *A Small Treatise on the Great Virtues: The Uses of Philosophy in Everyday Life* (Picador, 2002).

Josef Pieper, *The Four Cardinal Virtues* (University of Notre Dame Press, 1966).

Plato, *The Complete Dialogues*, ed. Edith Hamilton and Huntington Cairns (Princeton University Press, 1961).

Chapter 3: The intellectual virtues: being mindful

Julia Annas, *Intelligent Virtue* (Oxford University Press, 2011).

Audrey L. Anton, *The Bright and the Good: The Connection between Intellectual and Moral Virtues* (Rowman and Littlefield, 2018).

Quassim Cassam, *Vices of the Mind* (Oxford University Press, 2019).

Philip E. Dow, *Virtuous Minds: Intellectual Character Development* (Intervarsity, 2013).

Tom Nichols, *The Death of Expertise* (Oxford University Press, 2015).

Robert C. Roberts and W. Jay Wood, *Intellectual Virtues: An Essay in Regulative Epistemology* (Oxford University Press, 2007).

Linda Trinkhaus Zagzebski, *Virtues of the Mind: An Inquiry into the Nature of Virtue and the Ethical Foundations of Knowledge* (Cambridge University Press, 1996).

Chapter 4: Islamic and Confucian accounts of the virtues

Al-Ghazzali, *Alchemy of Happiness*, trans. Jay R. Crook (Great Books of the Islamic World, 2005).

Anthony Robert Booth, *Analytic Islamic Philosophy* (Palgrave Macmillan, 2017).

George H. Hourani, *Reason and Tradition in Islamic Ethics* (Cambridge University Press, 1985).

Philip J. Ivanhoe, *Ethics in the Confucian Tradition: The Thought of Mengzi and Wang Yangming* (Hackett, 2002).

Toshihiko Izutse, *Ethico-Religious Concepts in the Qur'an* (McGill University Press, 1966).

Jiyuan Yu, *The Ethics of Confucius and Aristotle* (Routledge, 2007).

Chapter 5: The theological virtues: be good, by God!

Augustine, *The City of God*, trans. Henry Bettenson (Penguin, 2003).

Romanus Cessario, OP, *The Moral Virtues and Theological Ethics* (University of Notre Dame Press, 2016).

Stanley Hauerwas and Charles R. Pinches, *Christians among the Virtues: Theological Conversations with Ancient and Modern Ethics* (University of Notre Dame Press, 1997).

Jennifer A. Herdt, *Putting on Virtue: The Legacy of the Splendid Vices* (University of Chicago Press, 2008).

Moses Maimonides, *The Ethical Writings of Maimonides*, trans. Raymond Weiss and Charles Butterworth (Dover, 1975).

Josef Pieper, *Faith, Hope, Love* (Ignatius, 1986).

Chapter 6: The capital vices: love gone wrong

Aquinas, *On Evil*, trans. Richard Regan (Oxford University Press, 2003).

Cassian, *The Institutes*, trans. Boniface Ramsey (Paulist, 2000).

Aaron James, *Assholes: A Theory* (Random House, 2014).

Rebecca Konyndyk DeYoung, *Glittering Vices*, 2nd edn (Brazos Press, 2020).

Solomon Shimmel, *The Seven Deadly Sins: Jewish, Christian, and Classical Reflections on Human Psychology* (Oxford University Press, 1997).

Gabriele Taylor, *Deadly Vices* (Oxford University Press, 2003).

Conclusion

John Doris, *Lack of Character: Personality and Moral Behavior* (Cambridge University Press, 2002).

Christian Miller, *The Character Gap* (Oxford: Oxford University Press, 2018).

Index

For the benefit of digital users, indexed terms that span two pages (e.g., 52–53) may, on occasion, appear on only one of those pages.